SARGONIC TEXTS
IN THE ASHMOLEAN MUSEUM, OXFORD

MATERIALS FOR THE ASSYRIAN DICTIONARY
NO. 5

SARGONIC TEXTS IN THE ASHMOLEAN MUSEUM, OXFORD

by

I. J. GELB

THE UNIVERSITY OF CHICAGO PRESS
CHICAGO, ILLINOIS

Library of Congress Catalog Card Number: 79–111601

THE UNIVERSITY OF CHICAGO PRESS, CHICAGO 60637
The University of Chicago Press, Ltd., London, W.C. 1

PHOTOLITHOPRINTED BY CUSHING - MALLOY, INC.
ANN ARBOR, MICHIGAN, UNITED STATES OF AMERICA
1970

TABLE OF CONTENTS

PREFACE

General Remarks

This volume presents Sargonic texts in the Ashmolean Museum, Oxford. Almost all of these texts come from Kish and Umm-el-Jīr near Kish. A few Sargonic texts of unknown provenience acquired by the Ashmolean Museum have been added at the end of the volume.

The one hundred and sixteen texts in this volume are divided as follows: seventy-one texts are from Kish, of which sixty-eight (Nos. 1-65 and 114-116) are in Oxford and three (Nos. 102-104) are in Baghdad; thirty-six texts are from Umm-el-Jīr (Nos. 66-101); and nine texts are of unknown origin (Nos. 105-113).

I became acquainted with the Oxford Kish texts in 1950 through the generosity of the late P. van der Meer, who placed a second draft of his copies of forty-three Kish texts at my disposal. Professor T. Jacobsen kindly collated a number of difficult passages in these texts in 1953. While in Oxford during the summers of 1965 and 1966 I discovered and transliterated many more texts from Kish, all the Umm-el-Jīr texts, and the small collection of texts of unknown origin. In the summer of 1966 I also had the occasion to study the Kish material in Baghdad.

The present location of van der Meer's copies of the Kish texts is unknown to me; they are presumably in Holland. The original plan to publish these copies in the series "Oxford Editions of

Cuneiform Texts" was abandoned by the Oxford authorities, who deemed them unsuitable for publication.

Because of their newness and importance, all the texts transliterated in this volume (with the exception of Nos. 1, 102, 103, and 104) are also reproduced in photographs on Plates I-XLVI, at the end of the volume. This was done not only to illustrate the epigraphic features of a new province of Akkadian, but also to provide a check for my transliterations of the texts. All tablets are shown in their original size, with the exception of the important incantation, Kish 1930, 143, which is reproduced in an enlarged form.

The lexical and grammatical items of most of the Kish texts published in this volume have been excerpted and utilized in *MAD* II and III, where they were cited by their Kish numbers. I have retained the Kish numbering in the citations and crossreferences used in this volume to facilitate the finding of corresponding occurrences in the *MAD* II and III volumes.

I wish to express my sincerest appreciation to the authorities of the Ashmolean Museum, Messrs. D. B. Harden, R. W. Hamilton, and P. R. S. Moorey, for placing the tablets at my disposal and for helping me in every possible way. My thanks go also to Professor O. R. Gurney and Mr. Peter Hulin for their kind cooperation. I feel grateful also to Dr. Feisal al-Wailly, the Director General of Antiquities in Iraq, and to Mr. Fuad Safar, the Inspector General of Excavation, for giving me access to the Kish materials and to the catalogues in the Baghdad Museum.

Provenience of Tablets

Questions of provenience will be taken up in the following order: Kish tablets, Umm-el-Jīr tablets, and the Ashmolean 1924 collection.

All information about the place of origin and find-spots of the Kish tablets has been excerpted from the Oxford catalogues, supplemented by catalogues in Baghdad and in the Field Museum, Chicago.

All the Kish texts were excavated at Ingharra, in the south-eastern corner of the Kish complex of mounds. "Ingharra" is the form I found most frequently used in the reports, although the Arabic form as cited in the reports is ʾIṅgarā (إنْغَرَى). I learn from McGuire Gibson that the spellings En-ʾUrrah and en-ʾUrrah were used in John P. Peters, Nippur I (New York, 1899) p. 323, and that the form Umm Gharrah was used occasionally in unpublished materials by Mackay, the excavator of Kish. None of the suggested Arabic interpretations of the name appeal to me. For the location of Ingharra, see Ernest Mackay, A Sumerian Palace and the "A" Cemetery at Kish Part II (Chicago, 1929) map facing p. 65.

Whenever known, the information about the find-spots (locus) of the Kish tablets has been included in the description of the tablets. Out of sixty-five Kish tablets at Oxford, the available information is limited to one tablet of Kish 1929, twenty-eight tablets of Kish 1930, and three tablets of Kish 1931.

The year noted after Kish, as in "Kish 1930," does not denote necessarily the year nor the season (such as 1929/30 or 1930/31) in which the tablet was excavated at Ingharra. It indicates the year it was accessioned by the Ashmolean Museum, which may be more than a year after the tablet entered the Museum. Thus I noted in the Accessions Register that fragments Kish 1930, 173a-c were excavated in the season Kish 1928/29.

Nos. 102-104, representing three Sargonic texts in the Iraq Museum, are said to come "from casual discovery in 1935 at Kish," according to the information furnished to me in a letter by Dr. Faisal al-Wailly.

All the past information available for the tablets marked in this volume as "Umm-el-Jīr 1932" gives Umm-el-Jerab, Umm-el-Djerab, Umm Jerab, and Umm Jirab as the site of the tablets. This includes the Oxford Accessions Register, the sigla on individual tablets in Oxford, and the correspondence file in the Field Museum, Chicago. The location of this "site in the desert" is given as eight kilometers five hundred meters, according to one unpublished report, and four miles south-east of Barghuthiat, according to another. For published reports, cf. S. Langdon, Iraq I (1934) p. 115, who speaks of the "rich archaeological area at Jamdat Nasr, a half mile north of Barghuthiat, and at Umm Jirab, 5 miles south of it," and A. Parrot, Archéologie mésopotamienne (Paris, 1946) p. 322, who refers briefly to "Umm Djerab, 25 km au N.-E. de Kish" (see also map on p. 321).

For a time I was baffled by my inability to locate the site of Umm-el-Jerab on any geographical map available to me. I soon discovered, however, that the Oriental Institute Survey map of Iraq, prepared by Robert McC. Adams, has "T. el-Jeir" (in Arabic Tall al-Jīr, with jīm) about eight kilometers south-east of I. (that is ʾĪšān) Barghuthiat, that is, exactly in the area where Umm-el-Jerab was supposed to have been situated according to earlier reports. This information was partially confirmed in 1966 in Baghdad by Fuad Safar, whose archeological map showed El-Jīr (in Arabic Al-Qīr) located some seven kilometers south-east of Barghuthiat. I could not confirm his information about the existence of another site called Tulūl el-Jīr (also spelled with qāf) situated three kilometers south-east of El-Jīr. Fuad Safar found no evidence anywhere about the alleged Umm-el-Jerab. The information brought back by McGuire Gibson in the spring of 1967 was that the name Umm-el-Jerab is completely unknown and the forms of the name which he heard from the Arabs were Umm-el-Jīr, Tell-el-Jīr, and even ʾAbū-Jīr. See also below. For all these reasons I have changed the name Umm-el-Jerab to Umm-el-Jīr. It must be left open for the time being whether the word jīr in the name stands for jīr (with jīm) "chalk" or for jīr (that is, qīr with qāf pronounced jīr) "bitumen."

Much scattered and confused information concerning

the site called Umm-el-Jerab, its excavations, and its tablets is to be found in the correspondence file of the Field Museum, including letters from Watelin to Langdon and from Watelin and Langdon to the Director of the Field Museum, dated from February to June 1932.

The letters refer to Arabs who had been digging there and finding tablets which they then brought to the Expedition. There is nothing clear in the records to provide evidence that tablets from clandestine excavations had been acquired by the Expedition. A letter from Watelin to Langdon refers to hearsay information that some of the tablets were on sale in Baghdad and that Thureau-Dangin and Contenau bought them. There is no information in the Louvre to substantiate the latter statement.

The actual dig at Umm-el-Jerab was started by Watelin on March 1, 1932 and lasted for about two weeks. There are brief reports about Agade inscriptions and tablets and seals of Agade found on the surface of the site. The letters make several references to sensational finds of Agade tablets with the apparent inference that Umm-el-Jerab (or, via some confusion, Barghuthiat, in one of the letters) is the site of ancient Agade.

Impressed by the importance of the site and especially by its tablets, I suggested to the Director of the Oriental Institute, Professor Robert McC. Adams, the need to explore the Umm-el-Jīr area. As a result, Mr. McGuire Gibson, a graduate student at the University of Chicago (now Assistant Professor of Anthropology at the University of Illinois Circle Campus in Chicago), was sent to Iraq, and in a joint Directorate General of Antiquities of Iraq and Oriental Institute of Chicago project explored the whole Kish area in December 1966. Gibson excavated parts of the mound of Umm-el-Jīr in January of 1967, finding Old Akkadian seals, but no tablets.

Several questions must be raised about the thirty-six tablets here published in the collection Umm-el-Jīr 1932. Were all the tablets in the collection excavated by the Expedition? Or were some of the tablets excavated, while others were acquired from the Arabs? How reliable is the information obtained from the Arabs that they had dug up the tablets on the site later excavated by the Expedition? And if the information is reliable, is there any guarantee that one or more tablets acquired elsewhere might not have been added to the Umm-el-Jīr collection, as so often happens with our field expeditions? There are no answers to these questions in the available records.

According to the Oxford Accessions Register and the sigla on the tablets, all the tablets here published under the collection Umm-el-Jīr 1932 have a notation "Umm-el-Jerab" or "Umm-el-Djerab" with the exception of four texts, which lack this notation. Of these four texts, two, namely 1932, 402 and 1932, 416, lack any apparent connection with the group as a whole, but are published here because they are Sargonic and because of the possibility that they may belong here on the basis of evidence which may be discovered when more tablets from Umm-el-Jīr become available. The other two texts, namely 1932, 413 and 1932, 420, have definite connections with the tablets of the Umm-el-Jīr collection.

Tablet 1932, 413 is linked with 1932, 527 by the mention of the geographical name Mugdan, and with 1932, 346 by the mention of the personal name PÙ.ŠA-ḪAL.

Tablet 1932, 420 is linked with 1932, 527 by the mention of Mugdan, and with 1932, 358 by the spelling _ub_-AN for _ublam_.

The important text Umm-el-Jīr 1932, 527 is linked with Umm-el-Jīr 1932, 348, and both these texts are connected with _BIN_ VIII 144. This is clear from the following:

PN _Ù-ì-lí_, Umm-el-Jīr 1932, 348 i 4', 11'; Umm-el-Jīr 1932, 527 ii' 6, 15 = _BIN_ VIII 144 ii 22, 29, 38

PN _Gi-nu-mu-bí_ DUB.SAR, Umm-el-Jīr 1932, 348 ii 7' =? _Gi-nu-mu-bí_ PA.TE.SI, _BIN_ VIII 144 iv 56

PN _Gu-gu-ša_, Umm-el-Jīr 1932, 527 ii' 1 = _BIN_ VIII 144 ii 27

GN _Bil$_x$-lum_-TUR^{KI}, Umm-el-Jīr 1932, 348 ii 8', and _Bil$_x$-lum_-GAL^{KI}, Umm-el-Jīr 1932, 527 ii' 14 = _BIN_ VIII 144 iii 37

GN _Mug-da-an_^{KI}, Umm-el-Jīr 1932, 527 ii' 10 = _BIN_ VIII 144 iii 33

PN _Lu-lu_ _it-ru_, Umm-el-Jīr 1932, 527 ii' 3
= _BIN_ VIII 144 iii 31

PN _Lu-lu_ _iš-lu-ul_, Umm-el-Jīr 1932, 527 rev. i
1f. = _BIN_ VIII 144 ii 16f., iii 39, 44

ŠE, ZÍD, $MUNU_x$.GAZ, Umm-el-Jīr 1932, 527 ii'
11-13 = _BIN_ VIII 144 iii 34-36

Thus _BIN_ VIII 144 clearly comes from the same site as the Umm-el-Jīr collection. The _BIN_ VIII 144 text belongs to the Collection of James B. Nies at Yale, and nothing is known about its provenience.

Many texts from Umm-el-Jīr have one characteristic which distinguishes them from Sargonic texts from other sites, and that is the form in which certain measures of dry capacity are written, namely x GUR ŠE SAG (Umm-el-Jīr 1932, 350, 359, 363, and 364) and x ŠE SAG.GÁL (Umm-el-Jīr 1932, 345, 349, 351, 353, 356, 357, 358, 361, and 366). Beside these measures of capacity limited to Umm-el-Jīr, other Umm-el-Jīr texts use standard Sargonic forms, such as x ŠE GUR (Umm-el-Jīr 1932, 348, 360, 369, 402, 413, 527, and _BIN_ VIII 144), x ŠE GUR _A-ga-dè_^{KI} (Umm-el-Jīr 1932, 367, and _BIN_ VIII 144), and x ŠE GUR.SAG.GÁL (Umm-el-Jīr 1932, 372b).

Nothing of importance concerning the provenience of the nine Sargonic texts added at the end of this volume is to be found in the catalogues of the Ashmolean Museum.

Date of Tablets

From the epigraphic point of view all the texts published in this volume belong to the Sargonic period, with the exception of a few texts which show certain older or younger characteristics. Thus the thick, roundish tablets Kish 1930, 173a, 173b, 173c, 347b, 559b, Kish 1931, 144c, and Umm-el-Jīr 1932, 369 show certain aspects of Pre-Sargonic writing; while Kish 1930, 177k and Kish 1930, 348b give the appearance of tablets of the Ur III period.

Since no tablet in this volume bears a year date, it is impossible to place the tablets exactly within the Sargonic period. However, the mention of _Sar-a-ti-gu-bi-si-in_ in Kish 1930, 170e 8 helps in dating the Kish tablets, just as the mention of _Gi-šum_ PA.TE.SI in Umm-el-Jīr 1932, 348 i 5f. helps in dating the Umm-el-Jīr collection.

Kish 1930, 170e 1ff. reads as follows: _Adī-ilum ištê Ilum-dan ši Šu-ilišu šassukkim wardi Ilum-bānî tamkārim wardi Sar-a-ti-gu-bi-si-in uššab_ "Adī-ilum resides with Ilum-dan of the clan of Šu-ilišu the field recorder, (who is) in the service of Ilum-bānî the merchant, (who in turn is) in the service of _Sar-a-ti-gu-bi-si-in_." Here the word _wardum_ obviously does not mean "slave" since slaves have no patronymics or professions, and the translation "servant" should be avoided because it means nothing. To me, the term _wardum_ denotes a socio-economic dependence of a lower-standing individual and his household on a higher-standing individual and his household. This kind of relationship is expressed by the words "sake and soke" in medieval English terminology.

The individual *Sar-a-ti-gu-bi-si-in*, who had under him the household of a merchant, who in turn had under him the household of a field recorder, must have been an individual of the highest class.

The name *Sar-a-ti-gu-bi-si-in* occurs also in a Sumerian votive inscription of one *Níg*-UL-*pa-è*, dedicated *nam-ti Sar-a-ti-gu-bi-si-in, lugal-la-na-šè* "for the life of S., his king" (or "lord") (*RA* IX [1912] pp. 73-76), and on a seal dedicated to *S. dumu lugal* "S., the prince" (R.M. Boehmer, *Die Entwicklung der Glyptik während der Akkad-Zeit* [Berlin, 1965] Abb. 271).

The name S. was explained as foreign, possibly Gutian, by Thureau-Dangin, *op. cit.* p. 75, and Poebel, *PBS* IV p. 135. Jacobsen, *SKL* p. 120 n. 308, interpreted it as possibly Akkadian *Muati-qu(b)bîsin* "Muati (has heard) their wail" and Gelb, *MAD* III p. 287, translated it as possibly "O king, I gave their (sisters') laments." Several scholars suggested that S. may represent the name, now lost, of one of the Gutian rulers in the Sumerian King List.

The main question pertains to the translation of *lugal* in the Sumerian votive inscription as "king" or "lord." Note that S. bears no title whatsoever in the Kish tablet and he is not said to be a *lugal* of a country in the votive inscription.

Considering the rarity of the name S. and the

very high position of S. implied by both our text and the other inscriptions, I have no hesitation in identifying him as one and the same individual. S. may well have been one of the powerful overlords, Akkadian or Gutian, who helped to bring about the downfall of the hegemony of the Sargonic dynasty during and after the reign of Šar-kali-šarrī, leading to the ensuing dark ages of the Gutian period.

If reconstructed correctly, the occurrence of *[um]?-ma-na-at* *[ma-ti* *G]u?-ti-im* in Kish 1930, 144a+b+c would add weight to the considerations in favor of the late Sargonic date of the Kish tablets, expressed above.

Qîšum, the ensi, occurring in Umm-el-Jīr 1932, 348 i 5, is found also in a Diyala Region text *MAD* I 161, in *A-ši-a-lí* DUMU *Gi-šum* DUMU *Be-lí-sa-tu* PA.TE.SI *Tu-tu-ub*[KI] "Ašī-âlī son of Qîšum, son of Bêlī-šadû, the ensi of Tutub," and in a text of unknown provenience, but perhaps also from the Diyala Region, Iraq Museum 43488, in *Gi-šum* *ti-na[m]* *i-ti-in* "Qîšum gave the judgment." The Diyala Region texts are dated approximately to the time of Narâm-Sin in the classical Sargonic period. *Gi-šum* PA.TE.SI DI.TAR "Qîšum, the ensi, the judge" also occurs in *BIN* VIII 121:12 and 18, a text of unknown provenience, but certainly of the classical Akkadian period.

The chronology of texts discussed above refers specifically to one or two (and other related) texts from Kish as dated to the time of Šar-kali-šarrī and afterwards, and to one or two (and other related) texts from Umm-el-Jīr as dated to the earlier time of Narâm-Sin. Obviously, no conclusions can be drawn from these considerations concerning all the texts from Kish and Umm-el-Jīr.

We find further help in dating the texts by observing the form in which the numbers are written. It has been noted for some time that in the classical period of Narâm-Sin and earlier the numbers are generally round, that is, they appear in the form of circles and semi-circles, but that they are often pointed in the later period of Šar-kali-šarrī and his successors, as in all later phases of cuneiform writing.

In observing the form of the numbers in the Kish and Umm-el-Jīr texts we reach some surprising conclusions:

About one half of the Kish 1930 texts use round numbers, while the other half use pointed numbers. The distribution can be easily observed on the photographs at the end of this volume. Thus the texts of Kish 1930 belong to the period from Šar-kali-šarrī on, when pointed numbers came into use. The late Sargonic dating of Kish 1930 texts confirms conclusions reached on the basis of the occurrence of <u>Sar-a-ti-gu-bi-si-in</u> in Kish 1930, 170e, and possibly of Gutians in Kish 1930, 144a+b+c.

All texts from Kish 1931 and Umm-el-Jīr use round numbers exclusively. This furnishes new information concerning the earlier date of the Kish 1931 texts and confirms the early date of the Umm-el-Jīr texts suggested above on the basis of the occurrence of the ensi Qîšum in Umm-el-Jīr 1932, 348.

Please note that the exclusive use of round numbers in standard situations is parallelled by the use of pointed numbers in special situations, even in the classical Sargonic period, e. g. in the texts from Gasur, the Diyala Region, and Susa. We find such uses of pointed numbers with MU "year" (Umm-el-Jīr 1932, 348 and 527), UD "day" (Umm-el-Jīr 1932, 358: 6, 8, 9), DUMU "son" (Kish 1930, 559a; Umm-el-Jīr 1932, 345 rev. i), DUMU.SAL "daughter" (Kish 1931, 121 i), GURUŠ "man" (Kish 1931, 121 rev. i twice), and with smaller measures, such as GÍN (Umm-el-Jīr 1932, 354 and GÍN.TUR (Umm-el-Jīr 1932, 363).

For further discussion of the use of numbers in the Sargonic period see <u>MAD</u> IV pp. xxiif.

Tablets

There is a slight difference in physical format between tablets from Kish and of the classical Sargonic period from Umm-el-Jīr. While the Kish tablets exhibit the standard Sargonic period format in having a flat obverse and a rounded reverse, a large number of Umm-el-Jīr tablets have both sides equally rounded. In addition, certain thick roundish-type tablets are characteristic of the older Sargonic or perhaps even Pre-Sargonic period; see above p. xvi.

Most of the Kish and Umm-el-Jīr tablets have one column, as is standard in the Sargonic period. Over a dozen tablets have two or three columns, and one tablet, Kish 1931, 122, has as many as five columns.

Writing

Several features pertaining to writing have been discussed above under the provenience and date of the tablets. These are: writing of dry measures (p. xv), general epigraphic features (p. xvi), and writing of numbers (pp. xix-xx).

According to the rule expressed in *MAD* II^2 p. 5, the vertical wedge in the signs ŠU, DA, and ID is pointed downwards throughout the whole Sargonic period except during the time of Sargon, when it is pointed upwards, as in the preceding Pre-Sargonic periods. The vertical wedge in these signs is pointed downwards in all the texts in this volume, with one exception. This exception is represented by Umm-el-Jīr 1932, 347, where we find the upward wedge in DA (i 1 and ii 3), ID (i 3), and ŠU (iii 4 and 7), but also the classical Sargonic downward wedge in ŠU (ii 2 and 9).

The sign BE with the value *ug*$_x$ in the writing of the personal name LÚ.UG$_x$.UDU (see Indices) and ÚŠ/UG$_x$ "dead" (Kish 1930, 406 passim) regularly has the expected form  , in contrast to  , which represents BE with the value *be*.

The clearly-written TI in TÚG.TI of Kish 1930, 170f may stand for BAL in the writing of the garment TÚG.BAL, well-known in the Sargonic period. Identical confusion of sign forms is attested in TÚG.TI of *MAD* IV 64:3, which clearly corresponds to TÚG.BAL of

MAD IV 69:3. The question of the sign form AM plus a vertical wedge for *am* in *a-za-am* of Kish 1930, 143:28 and 29 and of DUG plus a vertical wedge for *duk* in *Me-duk-la* of Kish 1930, 139:4 will be taken up, with many parallels, in the third edition of *MAD* II.

The comparison between *ub*-AN of Umm-el-Jīr 1932, 358:13 and 420:6' and *ub-lam* of Umm-el-Jīr 1932, 350: 7, and 11 and 359:6, 9, and 12 leads to the conclusion that AN has the syllabic value *lam*$_x$. However, the existence of *imḫurim* in *TCL* XXIII 96:7, Mari, for the expected *imḫuram*, may allow the consideration of the reading *ub-lim*$_x$, a form posited in my *Sequential Reconstruction of Proto-Akkadian* p. 125. Cf. also the feminine PN spelled ME-^{d}*Nin-su*-AN in Umm-el-Jīr 1932, 363:6, where too AN may be *lim*$_x$.

Note also the following occurrences of unusual sign forms and values: URU+TAR Kish 1930, 142:11; ZA-AR-KUG-PUM Kish 1930, 349b 3; the clearly-written SAR in *li-ti*-SAR of Umm-el-Jīr 1932, 360:6 leads to the reading *litîšar* (from *litajšar), a unique form in Akkadian, which may be eliminated by correcting SAR to IN yielding *li-ti-in* /*liddin*/, as in Umm-el-Jīr 1932, 354:9.

Umma influence can be detected in the form of the fraction for one-half in Kish 1930, 170f 2, Umm-el-Jīr 1932, 345 rev. ii 3 and 7, and Umm-el-Jīr 1932, 361:2.

Language

All Sargonic texts from Kish and Umm-el-Jīr are written in Akkadian, none in Sumerian.

The extraordinary preponderance of Akkadian versus Sumerian personal names, the occurrence of Akkadian geographic names, but of no clear Sumerian ones, and the exclusive use of Akkadian as the written language of the texts from Kish and Umm-el-Jīr confirm the ideas expressed in *MAD* II² pp. 11f. that the area of Akkade is thoroughly Akkadian in its ethno-linguistic aspects.

Of the nine texts of unknown origin, Nos. 105-113, four are definitely written in Akkadian (Nos. 105, 109, 111, and 113), two in Sumerian (Nos. 107 and 110), and three (Nos. 106, 108, and 112), in either Sumerian or Akkadian.

Almost all the names of the several hundred persons found in the Kish and Umm-el-Jīr texts are Akkadian, not Sumerian. Among Sumerian or possibly Sumerian names at Kish, note *En-kug*, *Dingir-gá*, *Igi-sig$_7$*, *Lú-kal-la*, *Lugal-iti-[da]*, *Ub-da*, and several names composed with *Ur-*, such as *Ur-si-gar*, *[Ur]*-^{d}KA.DI, etc. More Sumerian names appear in the texts of 1931 than 1930, especially in Kish 1931, 122. At Umm-el-Jīr I found only the names ME-^{d}*Nin*-SAR, ME-^{d}*Nin-su*-AN, and *Ur-kisal*, which could possibly be Sumerian.

Very important is the attestation of *E-la-an* MAR.TU "Ellān, the Amorite" in Umm-el-Jīr 1932, 350:2, because the name clearly corresponds to the Amorite name Ellān at Mari (RA XLIX p. 23) and Ellānum at Chagar Bazar (Iraq VII p. 37). A foreman called MAR.TU appears several times in Kish texts.

One of the most important contributions of the Kish and Umm-el-Jīr texts is the forty geographic names they mention. They shed light on the geography and ethno-linguistic background of Babylonia.

For the geography of Babylonia two texts are especially important, Kish 1930, 147 and Umm-el-Jīr 1932, 346. Both texts deal with fields located in different areas, and the geographic names mentioned in them must denote sites located in close proximity to Kish and Umm-el-Jīr, respectively.

The most common geographic name in the Umm-el-Jīr texts is Mug-da-an^{KI} (or MUG-da-an^{KI}), which occurs four times in three texts published here and in BIN VIII 144. On the basis of the frequency of occurrence it may be suggested that Mugdan represents the ancient name of Umm-el-Jīr.

The geographic name Gú-da-im^{KI} in Gen., occurring in Umm-el-Jīr 1932, 358:12, almost certainly represents the ancient Cuthah, normally spelled GÚ.DU$_8$.A^{KI}, located at modern Tell Ibrāhīm, which is situated about twenty to twenty-five kilometers north and northeast of Kish and Umm-el-Jīr.

Many geographic names in the Kish and Umm-el-Jīr texts are Akkadian, such as Bur-zi-da-an^{KI} /Pursîtān/, It-gur-da^{KI} /Itqurta/, and Ši-tu-ul-ni-šè^{KI} /Šitûl-nišē/. I know of no clear Sumerian names in these texts;

BÀD-^{d}EN.ZU$^{K[I]}$ is Dûr-Sin, GIŠ.KIN.TI^{KI} is Kiškattûm (cf. <u>Ki-iš-ga-ti</u> in <u>MAD</u> III p. 154), and URU-SAG.PA. ḪÚB.DU^{KI} is Âl-šarrākē. A number of names are clearly neither Sumerian nor Akkadian, but belong to the proto-population of Babylonia; such are, e.g., <u>A-ra-ga-zu</u>^{KI}, <u>Su-ur-gal</u>^{KI}, <u>Ti-me</u>^{KI}, and <u>Zi-na-e</u>^{KI}.

<u>Contents</u>

The majority of the Kish and Umm-el-Jīr tablets are standard administrative texts such as are found in other great collections of Sargonic texts from Gasur, the Diyala Region, Lagash, and Susa.

A small but important group of texts consists of contracts or memos concerning contractual agreements, such as Kish 1930, 170d (loan of barley), 175e (several loans of silver), 559c (purchase of a field), Kish 1931, 418 (purchase of a field), Umm-el-Jīr 1932, 351 (receipt of barley), 353 (loans of barley), 356 (loans of barley), 357 (loans of barley), 358 (loan and receipt of barley), 361 (receipt of barley as price of a house), 365 (loan of silver), and 367 (receipt of silver and issue of barley).

Letters and orders are represented by Kish 1927, 1, Kish 1929, 160, Kish 1930, 170c, 170e, 768, Kish 1931, 134, Umm-el-Jīr 1932, 354, 360, and 362.

School texts and texts with unrecognizable contents which may represent school texts are Kish 1930, 345d and Umm-el-Jīr 1932, 368, 369, and 370.

One of the most important texts in the collection is Kish 1930, 143, a beautifully preserved incantation invoking love-magic against a recalcitrant girl. This unique text is given below in transliteration and tentative transcription and translation. The differences between the interpretations here offered and those in MAD III are due to new collations of this difficult text as well as to several constructive suggestions received from Miss Erica Reiner and Messrs. Robert D. Biggs, Johannes Renger, and Aage Westenholz. I am also greatly obliged to Mr. Westenholz for his careful drawings of the cuneiform signs in this as well as in the MAD IV volume.

The eleven texts of the Ashmolean 1924 collection are all administrative, with the possible exception of Ashmolean 1924, 655, a memo concerning the exchange of four fields for oxen. Intriguing and difficult is Ashmolean 1924, 689 with its very high measures of surface.

Postscript

The manuscript of MAD V was already in the hands of the Editorial Office when I received a series of letters from Dr. McGuire Gibson with some new information about the Kish and Umm-el-Jīr texts. Dr. Gibson, a former student of mine at the University of Chicago, received here his Ph.D. degree in 1968 on the basis of his doctoral dissertation "The City and Area of Kish." In 1969 he left Chicago for Europe and the Near East on a one-year research trip to continue with his investigation of the archival materials of the Kish Expedition. While in

Oxford, he made a number of corrections and additions to my manuscript which I have been able to incorporate only partially in the main part. Other points are discussed below.

Dr. Gibson suggests that in order to avoid confusion I should stress once more (see above, p. x) that the tablet designations given in this volume, such as Kish 1929, 160 or Umm-el-Jīr 1932, 345, are in fact Ashmolean Museum accession numbers, not field numbers.

Dr. Gibson points out that the locus designation "Mound Z" was used by Langdon incorrectly and that it should be changed to the correct designation "Monument Z."

Dr. Gibson notes that the tablet Kish 1927, 1 carries a designation which was used by Langdon only in his <u>RA</u> XXIV publication. The whereabouts of the tablet is unknown, and the designation is neither a field number nor an Ashmolean Museum number.

By a stroke of luck Dr. Gibson discovered a number of old field photographs made by the Kish Expedition, which had remained unknown and unavailable in previous years in the Ashmolean Museum. A set of these photographs was sent to me through the kindness of Mr. Moorey. Some of these photographs show the tablets in a better state of preservation than they are now. These photographs, including No. 39 (Kish 1930, 348b), No. 45 (Kish 1930, 406), No. 47 (Kish 1930, 559b), No. 60 (Kish 1931, 134), and

No. 65 (Kish 1931, 418), are published on Plates XLIV-XLV near the end of this volume.

Three additional Sargonic tablets of the Kish 1924/25 season were discovered in the Ashmolean Museum and given the accession numbers Ashm. 1969, 562, 563, and 564. Especially important for the stratification of the site, according to Dr. Gibson, is Ashm. 1969, 562, since it forms "the basis for dating the 'Sargon Wall,' the supporting wall around the two ziggurats at Uhaimir."

As far as the philological content is concerned, the three texts offer nothing new. Almost all the personal names of these three texts find parallels in other texts from Kish. They have not been included in the Index of Personal Names.

The following transliterations were made directly from photographs, one set of which was made by the Ashmolean Museum, the other by Dr. Gibson. The Ashmolean Museum photographs of the three tablets are published on Plate XLVI at the end of this volume.

114. (Ashmolean 1969, 562)

1) [x]? G[UD N]a?-mu

2) 3? GUD A-li-a-ḫu

3) 1 GUD ⌈Ki⌉?-ti-ti

4) 1 GUD Be-lí-dan

5) [x GUD Š]a-aṭ-pum

(rest destroyed)

Rev. (beginning destroyed)

1') [x GUD ....]-⌈d⌉a-gal

2') [x GUD] ⌜Ì⌝-lu-lu

(space)

3') (destroyed)

115. (Ashmolean 1969, 563)

1) [x ŠE GUR PN]

2) [x G]UR Ì-lu-lu

3) [x G]UR É-ḫé-lum

4) [x G]UR KIL-DINGIR

5) [x GUR ....]-ì-lí

(rest destroyed)

Rev. (beginning destroyed)

1') [....] ....

(space)

2') [ŠU.NIGÍN] ⌜x⌝ ŠE GUR

116. (Ashmolean 1969, 564)

1) 1 DINGIR-su-dan

2) DUMU Šu-ì-lí-su ⌜KUG⌝?.GÁL

3) 1 Šu-ì-lí-⌜su]?

4) DUMU Ur?-.[...]

5) 1 Pù-su-[....]

6) DUMU DINGIR-⌜a⌝-b⌜a⌝

(rest destroyed)

Rev. (beginning destroyed)

1') 1 .[...]

2') DUMU DING[IR-....]

3') 1 .[...]

4') DUMU .[...]

5') 1 PÙ.[ŠA-^{d}Z]a-ba_4-ba_4

6') DUMU X?-ra-ra

7') [1]? Gi-šum DUMU Ì-la-la

The photograph of the reverse of No. 2 (Kish 1929, 160), reproduced on Pl. XLIV, was made by Dr. Gibson after he had found the missing chip of the tablet not shown on the photograph reproduced on Plate I.

Under the title "A List of Copper Objects" O. R. Gurney published Kish 1931, 128, a seven-sided prism, in *Iraq* XXXI (1969) pp. 3-7. The prism, excavated at Ingharra, is probably to be dated to the Sargonic period.

Dr. Gibson informs me that new information was discovered in the files of the Kish Expedition on the name, location, and tablets of Umm-el-Jīr. "Umm el-Djerab ou Umm el-Jir" is written in French in Watelin's handwriting on a sketch map of the Kish area, with Umm-el-Jīr in exactly the right location. According to Watelin's report to Langdon, "it is clear that he found a few chips of Sargonic tablets, but no substantial ones." See also pp. x-xv, above.

TEXTS IN TRANSLITERATION

ORDER OF TEXTS:

Kish 1927

Kish 1929

Kish 1930

Kish 1931

Umm-el-Jīr 1932

Kish IM

Ashmolean 1924

1. (Kish 1927, 1)

Data about the color, size, and present location of the tablet unknown. Text published previously by Langdon, <u>RA</u> XXIV (1927) pp. 90f. and 96. Letter of Qibî-Sin to Iliš-takal.

1) en-ma
2) Ki-bí-^{d}EN.ZU
3) a-na Ì-lí-iš-da-gal
4) ....-ad?
5) I-mi-DINGIR
6) DUMU Ni-si(g)-e-ni-sa
Rev. 7) DUMU.SAL I-lul-DINGIR DÍM
8) ARÂD Za?-....
9) li-⌈im?-ḫu?-ur⌉?

2. (Kish 1929, 160)

Light brown. 73 × 50 × 22 mm. Locus: Mound Z. Text published previously by Langdon, <u>EK</u> III Pl. XI. The first signs in lines 11-13, copied by Langdon, are now broken away on the tablet. Letter of Abbaja to Dudua. Plates I and XLIV; see also p. xxx.

1) en-ma
2) Ab-ba-a-a
3) a-na Du-du-a
4) mi-núm
5) ù-la a-bí ad-da
6) ma a-na 10 ŠE GUR
7) ù-la da-ki-ba-an-ni
8) É e-rí (or ʾà-e-rí)

9) šum-ma KUG.BABBAR

Rev. 10) è-rí-šu-ga

11) [a?-n]a? 20 GUR

12) [1/3]? ŠA GÍN lu-sa-bí-l[a]-kum

13) šum-ma ⌜a⌝-[na] SAG

14) [m]a? lu-sa-[bí-la]?-kum

15) [a]d-da šu-zi-a-am

16) [ù]? DUMU-ga ⌜šu⌝-up-⌜ra-šum⌝-ma

17) [su$_4$?-m]a? li-iš-me

3. (Kish 1930, 138)

Light brown. 56 × 42 × 18 mm. Locus: Y? Payment of one hundred and fifty gur of barley. Plate II.

1) 3(GUR) 2(PI) 30(SILÀ) ŠE GUR
A-ga-dè^{KI}

2) a-na iš-gi-ni GÁN

3) be-lu GÁN im-ḫur-ru

4) 62 ŠE GUR

5) A-mur-DINGIR

6) 45 ŠE GUR

7) a-na KUG 1(GUR) 2(PI) 30(SILÀ)
GUR

8) na-ti-in

Rev. 9) KUG-su 1/2 MA.NA

10) 40(GUR) LÁ 2(PI) 30(SILÀ) ŠE GUR

11) i-ba-šè

(space)

12) ŠU.NIGÍN 150 ŠE GUR

13) DINGIR-GÚ

14) a-na LUGAL É

15) u-sa-lim

4. (Kish 1930, 139)

Light brown. 57 × 43 × 14 mm. Locus: Y? Assignment of four individuals to two places. Plate II

1) 1 Ì-lu-lu

2) DUMU Eš$_4$-dar-nu-id

3) 1 Ša-aṭ-pum

4) DUMU Me-duk?(wr. DUG+) -la

5) a-na BAR^{KI}

6) 1 É-da-mu

7) DUMU Ì-la-nu-id

8) 1 Ì-lí-du-gul-ti

9) a-na A.ḪA^{KI}

(space)

Rev. (uninscribed)

5. (Kish 1930, 140)

Light brown. 71 × 47 × 16 mm. Locus: Y? List of eleven individuals said to be al "upon" eleven other individuals. Plate I.

1) 1 Da-da

2) al Ì-lí-dan

3) 1 Si-ir-ḫa-núm

4) al Iš-má-KÁR

5) 1 I-mi-^{d}EN.ZU

6) al LÚ.UG$_x$( ).UDU

7) 1 Šu-ì-lí-su

8) al ⌈I⌉-lí-lí

9) 1 GAL.ZU-DI.TAR

10) al Ku-ku

11) 1 I-bi-um

12) al Ip-šum

13) 1 Ba-ša-aḫ-DINGIR

Rev. 14) al Mu-tu-tu

15) 1 Ip-kum

16) al MAR.TU

17) 1 Sar-ru-ba-ni

18) al Su-ru-uš-GI

19) 1 Na-bí-um

20) al DAM.GÀR

21) 1 Iš-má-KÁR

22) al DINGIR-su-dan

6. (Kish 1930, 141)

Light brown. 32 × 28 × 9 mm. Locus: YW? Receipt of barley. Plate II.

1) 22(GUR) 3(PI) ŠE GUR A-ga-dè^{KI}

2) En-kug

3) im_x(DU)-ḫur

(space)

Rev. (uninscribed)

7. (Kish 1930, 142)

Light brown. 50 × 41 × 18 mm. Locus: Y? Lower part of the tablet destroyed. Assignment of nine workers to one place. Plate II.

1) [1 PN]

2) 1 Ḫ⌈a⌉-[....]

3) 1 Sá-lim-[a-ḫu]

4) 1 Zu-[zu]?

5) 1 Pù-zu-zu

6) 1 BALA-É-a

7) 1 I-mi-DINGIR

8) 1 Mu-lu-šum

9) 1 Iš-má-^{d}EN.ZU

Rev. (space)

10) ŠU.NIGÍN 10 LÁ 1 [GURUŠ]

11) URU+TAR ḪAR.S[I?-....] (not Ḫur-s[ag-kalam-ma])

12) [....]

8. (Kish 1930, 143+175h)

Light brown. 87 × 46 × 11 mm. Locus: Y? Incantation invoking <u>irʾemum</u> "love-magic," here personified, for help against a girl. This unique and important text is given in the following not only in transliteration, but also in tentative transcription and translation. Plates III and IV, enlarged.

1) ^{d}En-ki ir-e-ma-am
Enki irʾemam
"Enki loves

2) è-ra-[a]?-am
eraʾʾam
the irʾemum.

3) ir-e-mu-um DUMU ^{d}Innin
ir'emum mara' Innin
Ir'emum, the son of Innin,

4) in za-gi-[im? e?-ra?-a]b
in zaggi[m? erra]b?
enters? into the sanctuary?,

5) in ru-ùḫ-t[i ga-na]-ak-tim
in rûḫt[i kana]ktim
by the spume of the ŠIM.GIG
(incense)-tree

6) ú-da-ra wa-a⌈r-x (x) x⌉-da
udarra'? ....
he drives? .....

7) da-me-iq da-tu-⌈x⌉ da-pum$_x$(KA)
damiq .... ṭâbum
Good is the sweet .....

8) ki-rí-šum tu-ur$_4$-da-<am>
kirîšum ṭurdam
Send into the orchard,

9) tu-ur$_4$-da-ma a-na GIŠ.SAR
ṭurdamma ana kirîm
send to the orchard

10) ru-ùḫ-ti [g]a-na-ak-tim
rûḫti [k]anaktim
the spume of the ŠIM.GIG
(incense)-tree.

11) ti-ib da-ad-ga

ṭîb dâdka

Make happy thy lover.

12) a-ḫu-EŠ ba-ki ša ru-ga-tim

âḫuz pāki ša rûqātim

I seized thy mouth of far-away,

13) a-ḫu-EŠ bu-ra-ma-ti

âḫuz burrāmāti

I seized thy colored

14) ⌈e⌉-ni?!-ki

ênîki

eyes,

15) a-ḫu-EŠ ur_4-ki

âḫuz ûrki

I seized thy vulva

16) ša lim-na-tim

ša limnātim

of evil,

17) a-áš-ḫi-iṭ ki-rí-iš

ašḫiṭ kirîš

I leaped to the orchard

18) [d]EN.ZU

Suin

of Sin,

19) ab-tuq ^{GIŠ}A.TU.GAB.LIŠ
abtuq ṣarbatam
I cut off a poplar-tree.

Rev. 20) u-me-iš-sa
jûmišša
Daily?

21) du-ri-ì i-da-as-ga-ri-ni
dûrī? i(n)-taskarinnī
.... among my boxwoods,

22) ki SIPA ì-du-⌈ru⌉ za-nam
ki rēʾijum idûru? ṣaʾnam
as the shepherd ....s the flock,

23) ÙZ ga-lu-ma-sa U$_8$ SILA$_4$-⌈áš⌉
enzum kalūmaša laḫrum puḫādaš
(as) the she-goat her kid, (as)
the ewe her lamb,

24) a-d⌈a⌉-núm mu-ra-áš
atānum mûraš
(as) the she-ass her foal.

25) si-ir-gu-a i-da-su
širkuā idāšu
(Like) two strings are his arms,

26) X() ù ti-bu-ut-tum
.... u tibuttum
(like) a .... and a harp?

27) sa-ap-da-su

šaptāšu

are his lips,

28) a-za-am(wr. AM+𒁹) X() in
ga-ti-su

assam .... in qâtišu

a pitcher of .... is in his hand,

29) a-za-am(wr. AM+𒁹) i-ri-nim in
bu-ti-su

assam irinim in pûdišu

a pitcher of cedar is on his
shoulder.

30) ir-e-mu ú-da-bi-bu-si-ma

irʾemū udabbibūšima

The irʾemū have bewitched her

31) ù iš-ku-nu-⌈si⌉ a-na mu-ḫu-tim

u iškunūši ana muḫḫuʾtim

and made her ecstatic.

32) a-ḫu-EŠ ba-ki ša da-ti

âḫuz pāki ša dâdī

I seized thy mouth of love.

33) ^{d}Innin ù ^{d}Iš-ḫa-ra

Innin u Išḫara

By Innin and Išḫara

34) ù-dam-me-ki

utammîki

I conjure thee:

35) a-ti za-wa-ar-su

adi zawaršu

as long as his zawarum

36) ù za-wa-ar-ki

u zawarki

and thy zawarum

37) la e-dam-da

lā êtamdā

are not joined together,

38) la da-ba-ša-ḫi-ì

lā tapaššaḫī

may thou have no peace!"

9. (Kish 1930, 144a+b+c)

Light brown. 118 × 80 × 15 mm. Two-column tablet reconstructed from three fragments. Locus: Y? Rations of barley and distribution of silver to about forty-five individuals, of whom apparently only thirty-eight are included in the totals. Plate V.

i 1) [40(SILÀ) Š]E?-TA

2) [1 Iš]-má-KÁR

3) [DUMU] DINGIR-su-dan

4) [1] DINGIR-dan

5) [DUM]U? Ì-lí-dan

6) [1 Um]-mi-Eš$_4$-dar

7) [1 PN]

8) [DU]MU DINGIR-ga-lí

9) [1] PÙ.ŠA-^{d}Nu-ni

10) 1 PÙ.ŠA-^{d}Za-ba$_4$-ba$_4$
11) DUMU It-be-la-ba
12) 1 Ìr-e-pum
13) DUMU I-sar-ni-si(g)-sa-am
14) UGULA Ì-lí-dan
15) 1 DINGIR-su-a-ḫa
16) DUMU Ì-lí-lí
17) 1 Šu-[ì]-lí-su
18) [DUMU PN⌉
19) [1 PN⌉
20) [DUMU Su-r]u-uš-GI
21) [1] DINGIR-dan
22) DUMU PÙ.ŠA-^{d}Za-ba$_4$-ba$_4$
23) 1 Sá-lim-a-ḫu

ii 1) DUMU Ši-.[...]
2) UGULA Ku-ku
3) 1 Šu-ì-lí-su
4) DUMU A-li-a-ḫu
5) 1 I-bí-bí
6) DUMU Eš$_4$-dar-ni-sa
7) 1 Gur-bu-bu
8) [DUMU PN]
9) [1 PN]
10) DUMU Ti-[....]
11) 1 Na-bí-[um]
12) DUMU Ki-im-m⌈a-x]
13) UGULA Ip-šu[m]
14) 1 U-ba-ru-um
15) DUMU A-mur-^{d}UTU

16) 1 Ì-lu-lu

17) DUMU Za-rí-kum

18) 1 I-ti-ti

19) [DUMU PN⌉

20) [1 PN]

21) DUMU Ma-š[um]?

22) UGULA Mu-tu-⌈tu]

23) 1 U-[b]ar-ru-u[m]

24) [DUMU PN]

Rev. i 1) [1 PN]?

2) [DUMU PN]?

3) ⌈šu?-ut? zi⌉-im-d[a-tim]?

(double line)

4) 1 Gu-lí-zu[m]

5) 1 PÙ.ŠA-.[...]

6) DUMU ⌈I-ku?-$^{d?}$KA⌉

7) 1 Wu-zu(m)-mu-um

8) DUMU Íl-te-um

9) 1 É-da-mu

10) DUMU Ì-la-nu-id

11) 1 Iš-lul-DINGIR

12) DUMU DINGIR-[....]

13) 1 ^{d}IM-[....]

14) DUMU Rí-ig-mu-[um]

15) UGULA I-lí-[lí]

16) 1 ⌈PN]

17) 1 U-ba-ru-um

18) 1 DINGIR-ba-ni

19) DÍM

20) 1 Tab-su-ga

21) DUMU DINGIR-su-dan

22) 1(PI) 20(SILÀ) 1 Ki-[....]

Rev. ii 1) 1 Sar-ru-ru

2) 1 Šu-ì-lí-su

3) 1 Ga-zu-a-lum

4) [1] A-bí-DÙG

5) [1 ...].-DINGIR ŠU.ḪA

6) [1 ...].

7) [1 PN]

8) DUMU Iš-dup-DINGIR

9) za-gi-ru

10) 1 PÙ.ŠA-^{d}EN.ZU

11) DUMU Lu-ga-tum

12) 1(PI) 20(SILÀ) 1 $Eš_4$-dar-dan A.AZU

13) 30(SILÀ) 1 Šu-ì-lí-su šu LÚ.KAR

14) 1(PI) 20(SILÀ) 1 A-mur-DINGIR
DUB.SAR

15) ŠU.NIGÍN 40 ⌜LÁ? 2⌝? GURUŠ

16) ŠU.NIGÍN 1/3 ŠA MA.NA LÁ 1 GÍN
KU[G.BABBAR]

17) ŠU.NIGÍN 5(GUR) 20(SILÀ) ŠE GUR
(space)

18) [iš]?-tum

19) [um]?-ma-na-at

20) [ma-ti (or KAS+X) G]u?-ti-im

21) [i-tu-ru]?-nim (or [ip-ḫu-ru]?-nim)
(end)

10. (Kish 1930, 145)

Light brown. 58 × 43 × 10 mm. Locus: Y? Disposition of animals, barley, salt, objects, and a slave-girl in three places. It-ba-al, in masc., goes with A-mur-DINGIR; Eš$_4$-dar-É GEMÉ, fem., is one of the disposed items. Plate VI.

1) 1 AMAR.KIR
2) 20 UDU.ḪI.A
3) in URU-SAG.PA.ḪÚB.DU^{KI}
4) 10 ŠE GUR.SAG.GÁL
5) 5 GUR.SAG.GÁL MUN
6) in BÀD-^{d}EN.ZU$^{K[I]}$
7) 3 KIN.[....]
Rev. 8) 1 K[A?-....]
9) in Kiš$^{[KI]}$
10) 1 KUŠ.[....]
11) 1 Eš$_4$-dar-É GEMÉ
(space)
12) A-mur-DINGIR
13) it-ba-al

11. (Kish 1930, 146)

Light brown. 45 × 40 × 17 mm. Locus: Y? Assignment of thirty-two workers to four foremen. Plate VI.

1) 10 GURUŠ
2) UGULA I-da-DINGIR
3) 10 Ip-kum
4) 7 A-ḫu-ḫu
5) Ì-lí-GAL SUKKAL

6) 5 PÙ.ŠA-Eš$_4$-dar

Rev. (space)

7) ŠU.NIGÍN 32 GURUŠ

8) bi-ru

12. (Kish 1930, 147+175f+175g)

Light brown. 94 × 53 × 20 mm. Locus: Y? Location of ten very large fields in ten places. The total amounts to 3,132 IKU. Plate VII.

1) [2?(BURʾU)] GÁN

2) [SIG$_7$ ...].()^{KI}

3) [2?(BURʾU)] GÁN

4) [SIG$_7$ ...].^{KI}

5) [1?(BURʾU) 1(BUR)] GÁN

6) SIG$_7$ Bur-zi-da-an^{KI}

7) 4(BURʾU) GÁN

8) SIG$_7$ É-pù-a^{KI}

9) 2(BURʾU) GÁN

10) [SI]G$_7$ ⌈S⌉i?-ba-NI^{KI}

Rev. 11) 2(BURʾU) GÁN

12) [SIG$_7$ X()⌉-ga-ar^{KI}

13) 2(BURʾU) <GÁN SIG$_7$> Gi-⌈gi/zi⌉-NI^{KI}

14) 1(BURʾU) 4(BUR) GÁN <SIG$_7$>

15) Zi-na-e^{KI}

16) 6(BUR) GÁN

17) SIG$_7$ BÀD-da-mu-na^{KI}

18) 3(BUR) <GÁN SIG$_7$> It-gur-da^{KI}

(space)

19) [ŠU.NIGÍN 2]+1(ŠÁR) LÁ 6(BUR) GÁN

(=3,132 IKU)

20) [....] .[...]

13. (Kish 1930, 148)

Light brown. 58 × 42 × 18 mm. Locus: Y? Assignment of six workers to four foremen. Plate VII.

1) 1 Im_x(DU)-da-lik X()

2) UGULA Mu-tu-tu

3) 1 Ì-lu-lu

4) UGULA Ip-kum

5) 1 DINGIR-GÀR X()

6) UGULA MAR.TU

7) 1 DINGIR-GAL.ZU X(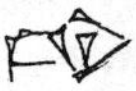)

8) 1 Ì-la-ag-nu-id

9) 1 Ì-la-la

10) UGULA Ni-su-dan-nam

Rev. (uninscribed)

14. (Kish 1930, 149)

Light brown. 51 × 40 × 13 mm. Locus: Y? List of five messengers under one foreman. Plate VI.

1) [1 La]-gi-pum

2) [1 L]a-ʾà-ra-ab

3) [1] ⌜Na?-ḫa⌝-DINGIR

4) 1 Pù-zu-zu

5) 1 Be-lí-^{d}EN.ZU

(space)

6) ŠU.NIGÍN 5 GURUŠ

7) Ì-la-ag-nu-id

Rev. 8) ìr-da-⌈ù⌉?( )

(space)

9) ŠU.NIGÍN 5 LÚ.KIN.GI$_4$.A

15. (Kish 1930, 150)

Light brown. 52 × 43 × 11 mm. Locus: Y? Bottom of tablet destroyed. List of fifteen workers called *wa-si-bu* "squatters," under one foreman. Cf. Kish 1930, 177n. Plate IX.

1) 1 La-gi-pum

2) DUMU Iš-má-a-ni

3) 1 Im$_x$(DU)-da-lik

4) 1 DINGIR-dan

5) 1 Ú-ì-l[í]

6) 1 Ú-ì-lí [....]?

7) 5 PAB.PAB

8) 1 Il-la-la

9) DUMU DIN[GIR-....]

(rest of obv. destroyed)

Rev. (beginning destroyed)

(space)

1') [ŠU.N]IGÍN 15 GURUŠ

2') UGULA E-lí-lí

3') wa-si-bu

16. (Kish 1930, 151)

Light brown. 40 × 37 × 13 mm. Locus: YWN. Assignment of two (or four?) workers to A.ḪA^{KI}. Plate VIII.

1) [1 X-x⌉-NI

2) [DUMU? B]u?-du$_8$-um

3) [1 B]u?-ra-núm

4) [DU]MU? Za-ab-tum

(space)

Rev. (space)

5) [a-na]? A.ḪA^{KI}

17. (Kish 1930, 152)

Light brown. 87 × 47 × 17 mm. Locus: Y? Receipt of barley (instead of silver) by nine bêlū "lords." Cf. also Kish IM 23302 end. Plate VIII.

1) [11 GÍN IGI.4].GÁL

2) [PÙ]?.ŠA-^{d}ME.SI

3) [10]+1 GÍN IGI.4.GÁL

4) ⌈Ì⌉-lí-BÍ

5) [10]+1 GÍN IGI.4.GÁL

6) [DI]NGIR-su-a-ḫa

7) [10]+1 GÍN IGI.4.GÁL

8) ⌈I⌉?( )-ba-LUM

9) [10]+1 GÍN IGI.4.GÁL

10) [Ì]-lí-iš-da-gal

11) [4]+3 1/2 GÍN

12) [PÙ.Š]A-^{d}Nisaba

13) [7 1/2] GÍN

14) Ì-lí-BÍ

15) DUMU Ì-lu-lu

Rev. 16) 7 1/2 GÍN

17) Ma-ga-ga

18) 6 GÍN LÁ 1 MA.NA.<TUR> 7 1/2 ŠE

19) PÙ.ŠA-^{d}Za-ba$_4$-ba$_4$

20) [DA]M.GÀR

(space)

21) [ŠU.NIGÍ]N 1 1/3 ŠA MA.NA 4 GÍN
1 MA.NA.TUR 7 1/2 ŠE

22) [be]-lu ŠE i-ma-ḫa-ru

18. (Kish 1930, 170a)

Light brown. 70 × 48 × 18 mm. Assignment of two hundred and seventeen workers to thirteen foremen. Plate IX.

1) 20 [GURUŠ]

2) UGULA Ì-lí-[d]an

3) 20 Iš-m[á-K]ÁR

4) 20 Mu-tu-tu

5) 20 Ip-kum

6) bi-ru

7) 20 LÁ 3 LÚ.UG$_x$(⊳+).UDU

8) 15 I-lí-lí

9) 15 Ni-su-dan-nam

10) 15 Šu-ì-lí-su

Rev. 11) 15 Ip-šum

12) 20 LÁ 3 Su-ru-uš-GI

13) 13 DAM.GÀR

14) 20 LÁ 2 ŠU.ḪA

15) 12 MAR.TU

(space)

16) ŠU.NIGÍN 180+30+[7 G]URUŠ

17) zi-me-id [LUGAL]?

19. (Kish 1930, 170b)

Light brown. 61 × 43 × 16 mm. List of six fugitive workers. Plate VII.

1) 1 Mu-tu-tu

2) 1 Šá-lim-a-ḫu

3) 1 Ki-bu-tum

4) 1 Ga-la-ab-É-a

5) 1 Iš-má-^{d}EN.ZU

6) 1 I-šim-É-a

(double line)

7) ŠU.NIGÍN 6 GURUŠ A+ḪA

8) UGULA Mu-tu-tu

Rev. (uninscribed)

20. (Kish 1930, 170c)

Light brown. 51 × 48 × 14 mm. Letter of Eštar-paluḫ to one or two individuals. Plate X.

1) en-ma

2) Eš$_{4}$-[da]r-ba-luḫ

3) ⌈a⌉-[na] Da-bí-bí

4) [ì-lí-d]u-gul-ti

5) [....]-ni-[?]

6) ^{d}⌈Ḫa⌉?-rí-im-be-lí

7) MAŠKIM

8) i-ḫu-uz

Rev. 9) DUB ša-a

10) Ú-gul-la-ni-su

11) LÚ.U$_x$(GIŠGAL)

12) li-iš-ru-ga-me

13) ù DUB a-ti-nu-šum

14) Ù DINGIR-su-a-ḫa

15) li-li-⌈kam⌉-me

21. (Kish 1930, 170d)

Light brown. 41 × 32 × 12 mm. Witnessed loan of barley by Adad-šar from Puzuzu. Plate X.

1) [x] ŠE GUR [A]-ga-dè^{KI}

2) ŠE É.SAR 1(BUR) GÁN

3) Pù-zu-zu

4) al ^{d}IM-sar

5) i-su

Rev. 6) na-áš LUGAL

7) it-ma

8) DINGIR-GÚ NAR

9) MAŠKIM

10) 1 It-be-la-ba

11) 1 Du-du

12) [1 Na]m-ri-ru-um

13) [1 Im$_x$(DU)-d]a?-lik

14) [1 Gur-b]u?-bu

U.E. 15) [1 SI].⌈A⌉-um

16) 1 Du-du .[...]

22. (Kish 1930, 170e)

Light brown. 38 × 29 × 11 mm. Order to return a man dwelling with Ilum-dan. Plate X.

1) 1 A-ti-DINGIR
2) iš-dè
3) 1 DINGIR-dan
4) ši Šu-ì-lí-su
5) SAG.DU$_5$
6) ARÁD DINGIR-ba-ni
7) DAM.GÀR
Rev. 8) ARÁD Sar-a-ti-gu-bi-si-in
9) u-ša-ab
10) li-ru-nim
11) DINGIR-GÚ
12) MAŠKIM

23. (Kish 1930, 170f)

Light brown. 37 × 30 × 15 mm. Bottom of tablet destroyed, but perhaps no more than one line missing. Disposition of silver, gold, garments, bronze vessels, etc. Plate XI.

1) [x] MA.NA 8 GÍN KUG.BABBAR
2) [2]+2 GÍN LÁ 1/2([sign]) MA.NA.TUR
KUG.GI
3) 3 TÚG.TI(sic)
4) 1 TÚG.DÙL
5) 4 UD.KA.BAR
6) [x X]
Rev. 7) [....]-rí-im
8) ⸢šu⸣-ut DINGIR-GÚ NAR

24. (Kish 1930, 170g)

Light brown. 30 × 27 × 13 mm. Receipt of barley by Naḫšum-pala᾿ from Iliš-takal. Plate XI.

1) 5 ŠE GUR.SAG.GÁL
2) in GUR.UL LÁ 2(SILÀ)
3) ša-ti 11 SILÀ-TA
Rev. 4) ra-ba-at
5) Na-aḫ-šum-BALA
6) ⌈iš-dè⌉ Ì-lí-iš-da-gal
7) im-ḫur
L.E. 8) in DÙN(=GÍN without GUNU).GAL

25. (Kish 1930, 173a)

Light brown. 37 × 38 × 20 mm. Locus: Y Red Stratum. Thick, roundish tablet. Distribution of sheep. Text similar to Kish 1930, 173b. Plate XI.

i 1) ⌈60? LÁ 1⌉ UDU
2) [Šu]?-^{d}En-líl
3) [ŠU].DU_8
4) [x UDU]
5) [PN]
ii 1) MU
2) a-na
3) MAŠKIM(wr. DU+KAS)
4) ŠU.DU_8
5) 1 (or 60) UDU
6) ⌈Pù?-pù⌉?
7) LÚ [....]
Rev. i 1) LUGAL

2) MU

3) ŠU.DU_8

(space)

ii (uninscribed)

26. (Kish 1930, 173b)

Light brown. 47 × 48 × 35 mm. Locus: Y 1 m. Red Stratum. Thick, roundish tablet. Distribution of sheep. Text similar to Kish 1930, 173a. Plate XII.

i 1) [x UDU]

2) [a-n]a?

3) KI.AN 3

4) 5 UDU

5) a-na

6) KI.AN 7

7) 4 UDU

ii 1) [....]

2) 2 UDU

3) Pù-p[ù]?

4) ŠU.[DU_8]

(rest destroyed; perhaps nothing missing)

Rev. (uninscribed)

27. (Kish 1930, 173c)

Light brown. 57 × 32 × 19 mm. Locus: Y 2 m. Red Stratum. Fragment of a thick, roundish tablet. Destroyed, but for one sign É. Plate XII.

28. (Kish 1930, 175b)

Light brown. 34 × 38 × 16 mm. Bottom of tablet destroyed. List of four messengers under four foremen. Text similar to Kish 1930, 175c. Plate XII.

1) 1 DINGIR-a-zu
2) UGULA I-lí-lí
3) 1 Ì-lí-TAB.B[A]
4) UGULA LÚ.UG$_x$([sign]).[UDU]
5) 1 Šu-ma-[za-ba]?
6) [UGULA PN]
7) [1 PN]
8) [UGULA PN]

Rev. (beginning destroyed; perhaps nothing missing)

(space)

9) ŠU.NIGÍN 4 LÚ.KIN.GI$_4$.A
10) a-na BAR^{KI}

29. (Kish 1930, 175c)

Light brown. 35 × 46 × 18 mm. Top of tablet destroyed. List of messengers? under foremen. Text similar to Kish 1930, 175b. Plate XII.

(beginning destroyed)

1') [UGULA] I-lí-lí
2') 1 Ì-la-la
3') UGULA Ku-ku
4') 1 DINGIR-su-a-ḫa
5') UGULA LÚ.UG$_x$([sign]).UDU

Rev. 6') 1 Iš$_x$(LAM+KUR)-e-si-na-at

7') UGULA Ni-su-dan-nam
(space)
(rest destroyed)

30. (Kish 1930, 175e)

Light brown. 25 × 37 × 13 mm. Top of tablet destroyed. Several loans of silver. Plate XIII.

(beginning destroyed)
x+1') E-da-⌈mu⌉ [illegible]
2') Su-ru-uš-GI
3') iš-dè
4') ARÁD-zu-ni im-⌈ḫur⌉
Rev. 5') 4 1/2 GÍN KUG.BABBAR
6') 1 MA.NA 5 GÍN E-da-mu
7') si-tum
8') a[l-s]u-ni
9') ⌈i⌉-[ba-šè]
(rest destroyed)

31. (Kish 1930, 175i)

Light brown. 37 × 42 × 6 mm. Top of tablet destroyed. Reverse of tablet flaked off. Account of barley. Plate XIII.

(beginning destroyed)
1') [NU]?.BANDA A-pu[m?-....]
2') ⌈30⌉ LÁ 3 SILÀ 1 Lugal-iti-[da]
3') DUB.SAR
4') 4(PI) 1 Ì-lí-bi-la-ni
5') DUMU En-kug

Rev. (destroyed)

32. (Kish 1930, 175j)

Light brown. 50 × 32 × 8 mm. Left and right sides of tablet destroyed. Reverse of tablet flaked off. Contents undefinable. Plate XIII.

1) [U]RU+A-ma a-[na]?
2) AL DAM .[...]
3) [i]q-bí-⌈ma]?
4) [ù]?-la u-zi-.[...]
5) [Na]-aḫ-šum-[BALA]
6) [x] BE [....]
7) [x?-x⌉ URU [....]
8) [x?-x⌉ TI [....]
9) [x?-x⌉ [....]
10) [i]n? URU.SAG.[PA.ḪÚB.DU^{KI}]

Rev. (destroyed)

33. (Kish 1930, 177g)

Light brown. 73 × 33 × 25 mm. Left and bottom of tablet destroyed. To judge from the greater thickness of the tablet on the left side, in comparison with the smaller thickness on the right side, the preserved part constitutes column ii of the tablet. List of messengers? under foremen. Cf. the similar text Kish 1930, 175b. Plate XIII.

(space)

ii 1) UGULA Ip-šum
2) 1 Gu-ra-tum

3) [DU]MU Á-a-pum

4) [1] DINGIR-a-zu

5) [DUM]U Ì-la-ag-nu-id

(space)

6) UGULA A-lí-lí

7) 1 Šu-^{d}Za-ba$_{4}$-ba$_{4}$

8) DUMU Igi-sig$_{7}$(IGI.GUNU)

9) [1 I]š-má-DINGIR

10) ⌈Zi-n⌉a-e^{KI}

11) 1 DINGIR-TA[B.B]A

(rest destroyed)

Rev. (one sign in one line preserved, rest empty space)

34. (Kish 1930, 177h)

Light brown. 34 × 44 × 20 mm. Bottom of tablet destroyed. List of fourteen workers under one foreman. Plate XIV.

1) 1 Pù-pù

2) DUMU I-nin-[nu]?

3) 1 PÙ.ŠA-Eš$_{4}$-d[ar]

4) DUMU DINGIR-a-z[u]

5) 1 Ku-ru-ub-Ì-<la>-⌈ag⌉

6) DUMU ⌈....⌉

(rest destroyed)

Rev. (beginning destroyed)

1') DUMU DINGIR-mu-[da]

2') in A-ga-dè$^{[KI]}$

(double line)

3') ŠU.NIGÍN 14 [GURUŠ]

4') UGULA A-ru-[ru]?

35. (Kish 1930, 177k)

Light brown. 45 × 45 × 13 mm. Fragment of a two-column tablet. The beginning of the horizontal dividing line clearly preserved in column i, just below SAG.PA.ḪÚB.DU. Reverse flaked off. Perhaps Ur III? Contents undefinable. Plate XIII.

i' (beginning destroyed)

1') [.....G]I?.ME

2') ⌈X⌉.ḪÚB

3') SAG.PA.ḪÚB.DU

4') UM+ME

5') AMA.GAN

(rest destroyed)

ii' (beginning destroyed)

1') KI[Š ....]

2') L⌈Ú ....]

3') LU? [....]

(rest destroyed)

36. (Kish 1930, 177n)

Light brown. 81 × 40 × 21 mm. Right side of tablet destroyed. List of workers called *wa-si-bu* "squatters." Cf. Kish 1930, 150. Plate XIV.

i 1) [1 Ku?-r]u-UR.SAG

2) DUMU ^{d}IM-sar

3) 1 DINGIR-su-dan

4) DUMU Iš-má-KÁR

5) 1 Ì-la-ag-nu-id

6) DUMU Ub-da

7) 1 Su-ru-uš-GI

8) DUMU I-bí-^{d}Nanše

9) 1 I-ti-ti

10) DUMU Im$_{x}$(DU)-da-lik

11) 1 SIG$_{5}$-DINGIR

12) DUMU DINGIR-ba-ni

13) 1 DINGIR-a-ḫa

14) DUMU A-ḫu-ni-si(g)

15) 1 Šu-^{d}En-líl

16) [DUMU] DINGIR-GÀR

ii (several lines with traces of signs)

Rev. i (destroyed, unknown whether inscribed)

ii (space)

1) wa-si-bu

37. (Kish 1930, 345d)

Reddish-brown. 33 × 33 × 10 mm. Locus: C 6, 2 m. Reverse uninscribed. Unreadable signs. School text. Plate XIV.

38. (Kish 1930, 347b)

Light brown. 32 × 45 × 11 mm. Locus: C 6, 4 m. Round tablet. Top of tablet destroyed. Contents undefinable. Plate XV.

i (beginning destroyed)

1') [...].

2') NU.MU.DU

3') 2 TÚG

ii (beginning destroyed)

1') ⌈x x⌉ a-na .[...]

2') in LÚ.ARÁD

3') LÚ Sa-tu-ì-lum

Rev. i 1) ⌈NU⌉.MU!.⌈DU⌉

2) [x] GÍN KUG.BABBAR

3) [a-n]a? GÁN ENGAR

4) [I?-t]i-ti

(rest destroyed)

ii 1) ⌈....⌉

2) DU[MU?....]

3) ša [....]

(rest destroyed)

39. (Kish 1930, 348b)

Reddish-brown. 85 × 40 × 23 mm. Locus: C 6, 7 m. Only left side of tablet preserved. Perhaps Ur III. Contents undefinable. Plates XV and XLIV; see also p. xxvii.

(beginning destroyed)

1') ⌈10⌉+10 MU.[...]
UD.KA.[BAR]

2') 20 SILÀ.BANDA.DA
UD.KA.BAR

3') 3 ḫa-[z]a-bu
UD.KA.BAR

4') ša-at A-d[a]?

UD.KA.BAR É..[...]

5') [x x⌉ UD.KA.[BAR]

6') [...]. 1/2 M⌈A.NA]?

7') [....] ⌈x⌉ [....]

(rest destroyed)

Rev. (destroyed)

40. (Kish 1930, 349b)

Reddish-brown. 40 × 42 × 13 mm. Locus: C 6, PL. Bottom of tablet destroyed. Text deals with a field. Plate XV.

1) 3(BUR) 5 IKU 20 SA[R GÁN]

2) Ìr-šum

3) ZA-AR-KUG-PUM (all clear)

4) šu E+PAB ARÁD.ARÁD

(rest destroyed)

Rev. (beginning destroyed)

(space)

41. (Kish 1930, 351b)

Light brown. 21 × 24 × 11 mm. Locus: C 5,3m. (4). Bottom of tablet destroyed. Account of sheep and goats. Plate XV.

1) 1 UDU

2) 1? MÁŠ

3) [S]I.A-um

(rest destroyed)

Rev. (beginning destroyed)

(uninscribed)

42. (Kish 1930, 399a)

Light brown. 26 × 22 × 11 mm. Locus: C 7, 4 m. Writing badly worn. Account of goats. Plate XVI.

1) 1 MÁŠ
2) 1 ⌈ÚZ⌉
3) [PN]
4) SILÀ.⌈ŠU.DU_8⌉
5) DAM.GÀR
Rev. 6) PA.TE.SI
7) im_x(DU)-ḫur
8) 1 MÁŠ
9) Na-bí-^{d}EN.ZU
10) 1 MÁŠ
11) LÚ É?..[...]

43. (Kish 1930, 403)

Light brown. 37 × 40 × 18 mm. Locus: C 7, PL. Roundish tablet. Beginning of a two-column uncompleted tablet. Account of flour. Plate XV.

i 1) [...]. ZÍD.AN
2) [.... ZÍ]D.KAL
(unfinished)
Rev. (uninscribed)

44. (Kish 1930, 404a)

Light brown. 32 × 28 × 7 mm. Locus: YWN. Distribution of barley for one individual and one pig.

Plate XVI.

1) 30(SILÀ) Te-mi-tum
2) 40(SILÀ) ŠAḪ.ŠE
3) UGULA.KAŠ
(space)
Rev. (space)
4) ITI Ti-ru

45. (Kish 1930, 406)

Light to reddish-brown. 91 × 81 × 20 mm. Locus: YWN, 0.50 m. Three-column tablet. Account of workers, dead and fugitive, in one year, in a place called Šitul-nišē. Plates XVII and XLV; see also p. xxvii.

i 1) 1 I-bí-^{d}Za-ba$_4$-ba$_4$ ḪAL
2) DUMU Pù-ni-a
3) UGULA DINGIR-SIPA
4) 1 Pù-ni-a ÚŠ
5) šu Ša-li-ba
6) 1 Gu-nu-núm ÚŠ
7) šu La-mu-um
8) LÚ.SIRIS
9) 1 PÙ.ŠA-Eš$_4$-dar ÚŠ
10) [šu? M]u?-rí-um
11) [LÚ.MUNU$_x$]?.⌈G⌉Á
12) [1 ....-u]m ḪAL
13) [DUMU? It-be]?-la-ba
14) [ši? Ì-l]í?-a-ḫi
15) [1 ...].-su ÚŠ
16) [DUMU? ....]-ba

17) [ši? ....]

ii 1) MÁ.LAḪ$_4$

2) 1 [ME]?-DINGIR ÚŠ

3) DUMU Ti-ru-um

4) UGULA A-li-a-ḫu

5) 1 Ku-ru-ub-Ì-la-ag ÚŠ

6) šu Ì-lí-be-lí AB+ÁŠ

7) 1 ⌈Nu⌉?-ni-da ÚŠ

8) šu A-na-d[a]?-rí

9) DUMU É-a-DÙG

10) 1 ⌈Šu⌉-ì-lí-su ḪAL

11) šu Šu-ma-za-ba

12) UGULA É-a-sar

13) ŠU.NIGÍN 8 GURUŠ ÚŠ

14) ŠU.NIGÍN 3 GURUŠ ḪAL

15) NU.BANDA I-lul-DINGIR

16) 1 Si-ir-ga-núm ÚŠ

17) [DUMU G]àr-[t]um SIPA ÁB

iii 1) 1 I-da-DINGIR ⌈ÚŠ⌉?

2) DUMU Gu-nu-tum

3) 1 É-da-mu ⌈ÚŠ⌉

4) šu Tab-ba-ba

5) UGULA DINGIR-mu-da

6) 1 Ì-lí-a-ḫi ÚŠ

7) šu Gàr-tum

8) ZAG.ḪA

(space)

9) UGULA Su-ru-uš-GI

10) 1 DINGIR-dan ÚŠ

11) LIBIR

12) 1 DINGIR-dan ÚŠ

13) šu Ma-ga-ga

14) ši Sar-ru-ru

15) 1 PÙ.[ŠA]-^{d}Z[a-ba$_4$-ba$_4$ X]

Rev. i 1) X [....]

2) 1 SI[G$_5$-DINGIR? X]

3) šu Su-m⌈u-DINGIR]?

4) 1 DINGIR-su-ra-bí ḪAL

5) šu ^{d}EN.ZU-iš-da-<gal>

6) UGULA I-bí-DINGIR

7) 1 É-da-mu ÚŠ

8) DUMU Ga-áš-tum-BALA (more plausible than Šim-tum-BALA)

9) 1 Íl-e-um ÚŠ

10) DUMU DINGIR-GÀR

11) 1 Ìr-na-⌈x⌉[(-y)]-núm [X]

12) 1 ARÁD-ì-lí-[su X]

13) PAB.PAB

14) 1 Zi-zi ÚŠ

15) GIŠ.TÚG.PI.KAR.DU

16) 1 DINGIR-ba-ni ḪAL

17) DUMU La-da-k[um]?

ii 1) [ši? M]u?-da-a?(𒀀)

2) [1 ....]-DINGIR ÚŠ

3) šu Im$_x$(DU)-da-lik

4) DUMU ši A-tu-tu

5) 1 Me-da-lik ÚŠ

6) šu Zu-zu

7) 1 Ḫu-zu-us-DINGIR ÚŠ

8) ARÁD LUGAL

9) 1 DINGIR-su-ra-bí ÚŠ

10) ⌈š⌉u Šu-ì-lí-su

11) [SI]PA ÁB

12) 1 [SI⌉.A-um ÚŠ

13) ŠEŠ DINGIR-a-zu

14) DUB.SAR

15) UGULA ⌈Ì⌉-la-la

16) 1 Be-lí-DÙG ÚŠ

17) šu Gàr-tum

18) SI[PA Á⌉B

19) UGULA ⌈I⌉?-[lul]?-DINGIR

iii 1) [1 PN X]

2) [....]

3) [1 ....]-dam? ÚŠ?

4) [1 ...]. ḪAL

5) [UGULA ....-D]I.TAR

(space)

6) [ŠU.NIGÍN 22]?+5 GURUŠ ÚŠ

7) [ŠU.NIGÍN 2]?+5 GURUŠ ḪAL

8) šu-ut 1 MU

9) in Ši-tu-ul-ni-šè^{KI}

46. (Kish 1930, 559a)

Reddish-brown. 39 × 32 × 12 mm. List of three workers called *za-bi-ù* *gi-nu-tum*. Plate XVI.

1) 1 I-kul-um

2) 1 Su-um-LUM

3) 2([sign]) DUMU Ì-lí-sa-liq

4) 1 DINGIR-ga-lí

5) DUMU Ku-⌜....⌝

Rev. 6) iš-dè

7) Ì-lí-sa-liq

(space)

8) ŠU.NIGÍN 3 GURUŠ

9) za-bi-ù

10) gi-nu-tum

47. (Kish 1930, 559b)

Light brown. 37 × 31 × 12 mm. Locus: YWN. Roundish in appearance. Contents undefinable. Distribution of one item each to three individuals. Plates XVIII and XLIV; see also p. xxvii.

1) 1 X ([sign])

2) Bí-bí

3) SANGA? X-y-z^{KI}

4) 1 X Y LÚ

5) .... Šu?-^{d}En-líl

Rev. 6) 1 X

7) E-x-y-um

8) šu? X-y-z^{KI}

48. (Kish 1930, 559c)

Dark gray. 42 × 45 × 22 mm. Top and bottom destroyed. Witnessed contract concerning the purchase of a field. Plate XVIII.

(beginning destroyed)

1') [a]-na ŠÁM GÁN

2') ši Za-bí-a

3') É.GI$_4$.A

4') da-áš-ku-ul

5') Iš-ku-DINGIR

(rest destroyed)

Rev. (beginning destroyed)

1') [....-LU]GAL?

2') 1 Ì-lí-iš-da-gal

3') DUMU DINGIR-su-dan

4') 1 Li-bur-me-šum

5') [....] SÀG

(rest destroyed)

L.E. [ŠU.NIGÍN] 6 AB+ÁŠ in Kiš[KI]

49. (Kish 1930, 559d)

Light brown. 59 × 33 × 12 mm. Top of reverse destroyed. Contents undefinable. Left fragment of the tablet now lost. List of men. Plate XVIII.

1) 1 DINGIR-su-dan

2) DUMU Ì-lu-lu

3) 1 Gi-šum

4) DUMU Ì-lí-dan

5) 1 U-ba-ru-um

6) DUMU [A]-ḫu-mu-bí

7) [1 PÙ]?.ŠA-[....]

Rev. (beginning destroyed)

(rest uninscribed)

50. (Kish 1930, 559e)

Brown-gray. 35 × 35 × 12 mm. Bottom of tablet destroyed. Contents undefinable. List of women. Plate XVIII.

1) 1 Zé-lí-tum
2) DUMU.SAL SI.A-⌈um⌉?
3) 1 ⌈Ì⌉-lí-a-bí
4) DUMU.SAL DINGIR-ra-bí
5) DU[MU ....-LU]GAL?
(rest destroyed)

Rev. (beginning destroyed)
(rest uninscribed)

51. (Kish 1930, 559f)

Brown-gray. 55 × 49 × 22 mm. Bottom of tablet destroyed. All personal names begin not at beginning of a line, but at a distance of one sign from the left margin. Contents undefinable. List of men. Plate XIX.

1) DINGIR-GÀR
2) Pù-Ša-mu-sa?(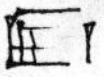) (or PÙ.ŠA-Mu-sa?)
3) E-ri-ri
4) En-na-na
5) PÙ.ŠA-^{d}EN.Z[U]
(rest almost destroyed)

Rev. (beginning destroyed)
(rest uninscribed)

52. (Kish 1930, 766)

Light brown. 57 × 42 × 21 mm. Only upper right part of tablet preserved. Account of barley. Plate XIX.

i 1) [x]+5(GUR) 2 2/3 [SILÀ ŠE] GUR

(rest destroyed)

ii 1) 44(GUR) 2(PI) 12 SILÀ ŠE GUR

2) É-maš-e

3) 53(GUR) 3(PI) [x]+6 GUR_8.SILÀ [ŠE]? GUR

(rest destroyed)

Rev. (uninscribed)

53. (Kish 1930, 767)

Light brown. 63 × 39 × 13 mm. Obverse (flat) side flaked off. The preserved side represents probably the reverse because it is slightly rounded on top and bottom. Contents undefinable. List of men. Plate XIX.

Obv. (destroyed but for the last line)

1') [1] Ti-r[u]-um

Rev. 1) [š]a Ti-ru-um

2) [1] ^{d}UTU-li-din

3) [1] Pù-su-DÙG

4) [1⌉ DINGIR-a-zu

5) 1 Ì-lí-dan

6) šu-ut I-da-^{d}EN.ZU

7) 1 ARÂD-z⌈u-ni]

8) 1 Ur-[....]

9) 1 PÙ.ŠA-[....]

10) [š]u-ut ⌈É⌉?-[....]

11) [1 Ḫ]u?-ḫ[u?-....]
(rest destroyed)

54. (Kish 1930, 768)

Very light to light brown. 48 × 35 × 14 mm. Letter of Warassuni to Tašmaᶜtum concerning two fugitives. Plate XIX.

1) en-ma
2) ARÁD-zu-ni
3) a-na Da-áš-má-tum
4) 1 Ìr-e-pum
5) ù 1 Bí-la-lum
6) LÚ.A+ḪA.ME
7) su-ma
8) e-la-ga-iš$_x$ (LAM+KUR = )
Rev. 9) za-ab-t[i]-su-⌈ni?-ti⌉?()

55. (Kish 1931, 86)

Light brown. 32 × 42 × 22 mm. Top of obverse destroyed. Account of sheep and goats. Plate XXIV.

(beginning destroyed)
1') ŠU.NIGÍN 60+2 U$_8$
2') ŠU.NIGÍN 1 ÚZ
Rev. (space)
(destroyed)

56. (Kish 1931, 121)

Light brown. 95 × 100 × 23 mm. Three-column tablet. List of thirty-seven GURUŠ and GEMÉ in the household of ^{d}En-ki. Plate XX.

i 1) [1 ....-š]a?
2) [1 Ra-b]a-tum
3) 1 Me-na-mu
4) 2( ) DUMU.SAL-sa
5) 1 A-li-li
6) 1 ^{d}EN.ZU-ni-⌈sá⌉( )
7) 1 Be-lí-BÀD-rí
8) 1 A-ma-.[...]
9) [1 W]u-zù[m-tum]
10) ⌈1⌉ ⌈É⌉-a-ni-⌈sá⌉( )
11) 1 A-li-li
12) 1 Na-wi-⌈ir⌉-tum
13) 1 Me-si-a
14) 1 É-a-ì-lí
15) 1 Ì-lí-lí
16) 1 Da-wi-ra
17) 1 GIGIR( )-la
ii 1) 1 MES( )-ti-bu [? perhaps nothing; narrow space]
2) 1 Da-li-bí
3) 1 Na-mu-ra-zu
4) 1 Rí-iš-tum
5) 1 A-mur?-DÙG
6) DUMU.SAL-sa
7) 1 Da-ni-a
8) [1 ....]-⌈SIPA-ì⌉
[(space)]
9) ŠU.NIGÍN 23 GEMÉ

(space)

10) 1 Šu-ì-lí-su

11) DUMU Eš$_4$-dar-BÀD-rí

12) 1 Pù-zu-zu

13) ŠEŠ?( )-su

14) 1 Gal-pum

15) DUMU Du-li-li

iii 1) [1 PN]

2) 1 [PN]

3) 1 Iš-má-^{d}[....]

4) 1 É-a-UR.SAG

5) 1 É-a-sar

6) DUMU Da-wi-ra

(space)

7) [ŠU.NIGÍN 8 DU]MU.DUMU

8) [PN]

9) NAGAR

(space)

10) ŠU.NIGÍN 23 GEMÉ 8 DUMU.DUMU

11) 1 NAGAR

12) iš-dè

13) I-mi-DINGIR

Rev. i 1) SABRA.É

2) 1 SI.A-um

3) 1 MES-šu-a

4) 1 Ur-si-gar

5) 3( ) GURUŠ in ERÍN

6) 1 Ša-aṭ-pum

7) 1 Bu-ga-núm

8) 2(𒐖) GURUŠ iš-dè
9) [PN]
(space)
10) GÚ.AN.ŠÈ 40 LÁ 3 GURUŠ.GEMÉ
11) ARÁD ^{d}En-ki
ii (uninscribed)
iii (uninscribed)

57. (Kish 1931, 122)

Light brown. 141 × 143 × 25 mm. Locus: C 10 (5). Five-column tablet. Text difficult to read. List of one hundred and thirty-eight male individuals. Plates XXI and XXII.

i 1) [1 ...].
2) [1 ....]-a?
3) [1 ....]-tim?
4) [1 ....]-⌈d⌉KA
5) [1 ....]-GAL?
6) 1 ⌈Ur⌉-^{d}⌈Utu⌉
7) 1 Lú-kal-la
8) 1 I-bí-zu
9) 1 Íl?
10) 1 Da-ti
11) 1 Me-da-lik
12) 1 Ì-lí-en-nu
13) 1 Be-lí-ba-lik
14) 1 Ì-lí-a-ḫi
15) 1 DINGIR-GÚ
16) 1 GAL.ZU

17) 1 Su$_4$-be-la

18) 1 ⌈I⌉?-ti-dam

19) [1 É⌉-da-mu

20) [1 I]-da-DINGIR

21) [1 I-t]i-DINGIR

22) [1 ....]-ad

23) [1 ....]-DINGIR

24) [1 ....-K]A?

ii 1) 1 DINGIR-dan

2) 1 Ì-lí-dan

3) 1 NÍG- 

4) 1 Ip-ḫur-⌈....⌉

5) 1 I-ku-^{d}Ìr-ra

6) 1 It-be-⌈ba⌉-la

7) [1 U]-za-si-⌈na-at⌉

8) [1] Gal-pum

9) [1 Iš⌉-dup-pum

10) 1 ⌈....⌉-ki-ág?

11) 1 B[u]?-ga-núm

12) 1 Ur-⌈keš⌉?^{KI}

13) 1 La-bi-bu?-um

14) 1 Ša-a[d]-mu

15) 1 Sag-gul-lum

16) 1 Ra-ši-ši

17) 1 [....]

18) 1 [....]

19) 1 [....]

20) 1 [....]

21) 1 AMAR.D[A]?

22) [1 R]a?-ḫi-um

23) [1 PÙ.ŠA]?-Eš$_4$-dar

iii 1) 1 Su-[....]

2) ni-ši [....]

3) 1 ^{d}ŠE[Š.KI-....]

4) 1 [....]

5) 1 [....]

6) 1 I-[....]

7) K[A ....]

8) 1 Ur-[....]

9) 1 Ur-.[...]

10) 1 Ḫa-r[a-x]

11) IGI.GUNU [....]

12) 1 Ir-[....]

13) 1 .[...]

14) IGI.GUNU [....]-KI

15) 1 Iš$_x$([L]AM+KUR)-gi-u[m]

16) 1? Ur-s[ag-x]

17) 1? Ur?-[....]

18) [1 ....-L]UM

19) [1 U]-ba-ru-um

20) 1 Al-lu-lu

21) 1 Sá-ki-ki

22) 1 PÙ.ŠA-⌜ru⌝-ru

iv 1) [....]

2) [....]

3) [....]

4) [....]

5) [....]

6) [....]

7) [....]

8) [....]

9) 1 GAL?-[....]

10) 1 En-.[...]

11) [1] ⸢....⸣

12) [1 ....]

13) [1] .[...]

14) 1 É-⸢bi⸣

15) 1 [Ì]-lí-sa-liq

16) 1 Im_x(DU)-da-lik

17) 1 I-ti-ti

18) 1 A-ḫu-DÙG

19) 1 A-ḫu-DINGIR

20) 1 UN.Í[L]

21) 1 Mi-sa-r[u]?

22) 1 Ki-.[...]

v 1) [1 X]-NI-[....]

2) [1 X]-ba-.[...]

3) [....]

4) [....]

5) [....]

6) [....]

7) 1 [....]

8) 1 [....]

9) [....]

10) [....]

11) [1 ...].[....]

12) [1 ...].[....]

13) [1 ...].[....]

14) 1 ^{d}KA-....]

15) 1 ^{d}[....]

16) [1 SI].A-um

17) [x M]U Ì.GÁL

18) [....]

19) [....]

20) [....]

21) [....]

Rev. i 1) [1 ....]

2) [1 ....]

3) 1 [....]

4) 1 Na-.[...]

5) 1 DINGIR-ga-lí

6) 1 Ba-tum

7) 1 Ig-⌈....⌉

8) 1 ⌈X⌉-é-ni-šè

9) 1 Šu-.[...]

10) 1 Ši-.[...]

11) 1 ÍL

12) [1 U⌉r-^{d}I[M]?

13) [1 É⌉-si

14) 1 PÙ.ŠA-[....]

15) 1 EN-l[i]?

16) 1 Ma-[....]

17) 1 DINGIR-[....]

18) [x]? 1 Lá-[....]

19) [1] Da-ak-[....]?-
mu-u[m]?

ii 1) 1 [....]

2) 1 I-nin-la-ba

3) 1 ⌜É⌝?-Me-me

4) 1 PÙ.ŠA-X( )

5) [1? L]i?-l[i]?

6) ⌜....⌝-su-rí-ik

7) Zi?-gur$_8$?-sa

8) Me-⌜....⌝.AMA ⌜....⌝

9) Pù-sar

10) 1 Šu-ra?

11) La-ni-m[u]?

12) $^{⌜d⌝}$Utu-ki-ág

13) I-ti-^{d}A-⌜ba$_4$⌝?

(space)

14) ŠU.NIGÍN 140 LÁ 2

(other columns uninscribed)

58. (Kish 1931, 130)

Light brown. 117 × 73 × 27 mm. Large fragment of a two (or more) column tablet. To judge from the context, probably the reverse of the tablet. Obverse almost completely flaked off. List of GURUŠ under foremen. Plate XXIII.

Rev. i (only ▷ and traces of signs for PNs are preserved)

ii (beginning destroyed)

1') [ŠU.NIGÍN x]+10 LÁ 1 GURUŠ

2') [G]ur-bu-bu

(space)

3') [ŠU.NIGÍN x]+42 GURUŠ

4') [....]-UŠ

5') [PA.A]L.É

(space)

(end?)

59. (Kish 1931, 133)

Reddish-brown. 54 × 50 × 20 mm. Only right side of tablet preserved. The attempted reconstruction of the beginnings of the lines is based on the thickness of the tablet. Account of barley. Plate XXIV.

(beginning destroyed)

1') [x Š]E GUR

2') [E]?-la-ga-lí

3') [x]+1 ŠE GUR

4') ⌈I⌉-ti-DINGIR

5') [x]+1 ŠE GUR

6') [Su]?-mu-GI

7') [x]+1 ŠE GUR

8') [I]-bí-u[m]

9') [x ŠE GUR]

Rev. 10') [X-x⌉-m[á?-....]

11') [x] ŠE GUR

12') [Ì-l]í?-SIPA

13') [x]+1 ŠE GUR

14') [Ur⌉-^{d}KA.DI

15') [x] ŠE GUR [....]-la

16') [x] ŠE GUR PÙ.ŠA-^{d}IM

17') [x ŠE G]UR Dingir-gá

18') [x ŠE GUR] Ga-li-l[i]
(rest destroyed)

60. (Kish 1931, 134)

Reddish-brown. 33 × 30 × 8 mm. Memorandum about a slave-girl and two or three persons. Since the interpretation of <u>ù-ḫa-za-za</u> as <u>*uḫassas-ša</u> for <u>*uḫassas-ši</u> "I am concerned about her" has its difficulties (morphemic and semantic), we may have to read <u>ù Ḫa-za-za</u> and interpret it as a PN to be added after lines 6 or 7; in favor of this interpretation note <u>è-la-ku</u> in Pl., rather than <u>è-la-ga</u> in Du. Plates XXIV and XLIV; see also p. xxvii.

1) 1 Te-mi-tum
2) GEMÉ I-lul-DINGIR
3) [DU]MU En-na-DINGIR
4) in A-⌈ga?-dè⌉?[KI]
5) wu-⌈ú⌉-r[a]?-at
Rev. 6) ARÀD-zu-ni
7) ù Ìr-su-tum
8) 2 ŠEŠ I-lul-DINGIR
9) KI Lu-lu a-na Kiš[KI]
10) è-la-ku
11) ù-ḫa-za-za

61. (Kish 1931, 136)

Reddish-brown. 58 × 40 × 25 mm. Fragment. All edges destroyed. Distribution of fish, flour, etc. Plate XXV.

(beginning destroyed)

1') [...]. .[...]

2') [X-a]n-.[...]

3') [x PI]SAN+GI KU_6.UD GAL

4') [x PI]SAN+GI KU_6 Ti-ga-lí
   1 TÚ[G]

5') ⌈Ì⌉-za-n[i]?

6') šu A-mur-D[INGIR]

7') 1 PISAN+GI KU_6.[X]?

8') 1 KUŠ.A.LÁ.GÁ ZÍD.[ŠE]?

9') [Ì]r-su-t[um]?

10') [...]. .[...]

11') [....] SI [....]

(rest destroyed)

Rev. (practically destroyed)

(only PISAN+GI readable)

62. (Kish 1931, 143)

Light and reddish-brown. 72 × 47 × 16 mm. Left edge is broken away so that it is impossible to see clearly how much is missing in front of some lines. List of personal names. Plate XXV.

1) [....]

2) Ib-ni-DINGIR

3) I-sar-um

4) (space) ⌈Zi-ra⌉?

5) (space) DINGIR-ba-ni

6) A-mur-ru-k[i?-m]a?-DINGIR

7) (space) Bu-BALA

8) PÙ.ŠA-Ma-ma

9) PÙ.ŠA-^{d}Za-ba$_4$-ba$_4$

10) [PÙ.Š]A-Ma-⌈ma⌉

11) ⌈Iš?-má⌉?-Eš$_4$-dar

12) [D]a-ba-ba

13) (space) ⌈A⌉?-ku-DINGIR

14) Su?-NI-um

15) Ì-la-la

16) [...].-sa?-ma-[x]?

Rev. 17) [DINGIR]-mu-da

18) Iš?-má-<Eš$_4$>-dar?

19) ⌈É-a⌉-ra-bí

20) Ti-⌈ti⌉?

21) Ma-⌈šum⌉

22) Ì-lí-BALA

23) DINGIR-mu-[da]

24) ⌈I-nin?-um⌉?

25) Ra-⌈bí⌉-DINGIR

26) A-ku-DINGIR

27) Bu-BALA

28) SIG$_5$-[DINGIR]?

29) [Šu-ì]-lí-su

30) [M]a-la-su?

31) [...].

63. (Kish 1931, 144a)

Light gray. 33 × 30 × 11 mm. Locus: YWN .01 m. Account of wool and lambs. Plate XXVI.

1) 1 GÚ 4 MA.NA SÍG

2) 10 LÁ 1 $SILA_4$

3) 12 $SILA_4$.SAL

Rev. (1-2 lines destroyed)

1') šu-ut I-tu-[tu]?

64. (Kish 1931, 144c)

Light brown. 30 × 48 × 12 mm. Locus: C 7 or YWN .01 m. Fragment of an at least three-column tablet. Reverse flaked off. Epigraphically, the text appears to be older than others in this collection. Writing GUR ŠE GÁL SAG, for the standard Sargonic ŠE GUR.SAG. GÁL, is unique. Account of barley. Plate XXIV.

i' (beginning destroyed)

1') [....]-TI

(rest destroyed)

ii' (beginning destroyed)

1') [x GUR] ŠE GÁL SAG

2') È-mi-^{d}EN.ZU

3') 8(GUR) 2(PI) GUR ŠE GÁL SAG

4') IGI-TIM-ZU

5') [x]+3(GUR) 1+[x(PI) GUR ŠE GÁL SAG]

(rest destroyed)

iii' (beginning destroyed)

1') NI-[....]

2') 7(GUR) [1]+1(PI) [GUR ŠE] GÁL S[AG]

3') Su-mu-DI[NGIR]

4') 4+[x GUR ŠE GÁL SAG]

(rest destroyed)

Rev. (destroyed)

65. (Kish 1931, 418)

Dark brown. 85 × 42 × 22 mm. Witnessed contract concerning the purchase of a field. Plates XXVI and XLIV; see also p. xxviii.

1) 2 GÍN KU[G.BABBAR]
2) a-na NÍG.ŠÁM GÁN
3) IGI na-ra-tim
4) Zi-ra
5) DUMU Bur-zum
6) im-ḫur
7) DINGIR-su-dan
8) DUMU I-mi-DINGIR
9) i-ti-in
10) in É-ti
11) Gu-lí-lí
12) DUMU.SAL ^{d}EN.ZU-al-su
13) in A-ga-dè^{KI}
14) 1 Da-kum
15) šu Da-da
16) 1 Be-l⸢í-a?-ḫi? DUMU I⸣-mi-zu

Rev. 17) [1 PN]
18) [DUMU? ....]-ri-DINGIR
19) [1 PN DUMU]? ⸢Ku?-ku?-zi⸣?
20) 1 [PN]
21) 1 [PN]
22) [1 ....]
23) .[...]-al-[su]?

24) 1 ⌈X-x-x⌉

25) ⌈DUMU? X-ni-x⌉

26) [1 PN]

27) [....]

28) 1 [PÙ.ŠA]?-^{d}Nisaba

29) DUMU Ni-na-⌈....⌉

30) .[...]

(double line)

31) ŠU.NIGÍN ⌈10⌉ AB+ÁŠ

32) DINGIR-su-dan

33) in [A]-ga-dè$^{[KI]}$

34) KUG.BABBAR iš$_{x}$(LAM+KUR)-ku-⌈lu⌉

66. (Umm-el-Jīr 1932, 345)

Reddish-brown. 97 × 106 × 24 mm. Three-column tablet. Memo concerning the witnessed receipt of barley (silver and other commodities) for thirteen fields, two loans, and three houses by twenty (thirteen plus two plus five) individuals, and the issue of barley to two individuals; apparently a composite memo concerning different transactions of one unnamed individual or household. Plates XXVII and XXVIII.

i 1) [x]+1(GUR) Š[E SAG.GÁL]

2) Im-gu[r-^{d}]EN.ZU

3) 10(GUR) ŠE SAG.GÁL

4) I-lul-DINGIR

5) NU.BANDA

6) 10(GUR) ŠE SAG.GÁL

7) Ì-lí-BÍ

8) 1 ḪA.GUNU.[SIG$_4$]?

9) Im-⌈....⌉

10) KUG 4 GÍN 10 UDU

11) Ar-ku-ma-BALA

ii 1) [....]

2) ⌈Z⌉a-na-d⌈a⌉

3) DUMU ^{d}KA-Me-ir

4) KUG 10 <GÍN> a-na Su$_4$-ma-DINGIR

5) 80(GUR) ŠE SAG.GÁL

6) DINGIR-ba-a (clear)

7) 33+⌈2⌉(GUR) ŠE SAG.GÁL

8) Ìr-su-tu-um

9) 20(GUR) ŠE SAG.GÁL

10) Da-ba-ba

11) 20(GUR) ŠE SAG.GÁL

iii 1) [PN]

2) [x(GUR) ŠE SAG.GÁL]

3) Šu( )-ì-lí-s[u]

4) DUMU En-bu-DINGIR

5) 10(GUR) ŠE SAG.GÁL

6) DINGIR-ag-nu-id()

7) DUMU É-a-dan

8) a-na ŠÁM GÁN

9) im-ḫu-ru

10) 20(GUR) ŠE SAG.GÁL

11) Zu-zu

12) ḫu-bu-lum

Rev. i 1) 5(GUR) ŠE SAG.GÁL

2) DINGIR-nu-id(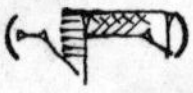)

3) ḫu-bu-lum
4) 20(GUR) ŠE SAG.GÁL
5) a-na ŠÁM 2 SAR É
6) ⌈I⌉-wi-ir-mu-bí
7) DINGIR-la-ag-nu-id( )
8) Šu-ì-lí-su
9) 3( ) DUMU.DUMU ⌈É⌉-a-da[n]
10) [im-ḫ]u-r[u]
ii 1) 5(GUR) ŠE SAG.GÁL
2) a-na ŠÁM É
3) 1/2( ) SAR
4) Zu-zu
5) DUMU Ti-ti
6) Ì KA GA[R]( )
7) KUG.BABBAR 1 1/2( ) GÍN
8) Ì ŠÁM 1 GÍN
9) 7(GUR) 2(PI) ŠE SAG.GÁL
10) a-na ŠÁM 1 É SAR
11) Pù-p[ù]
12) [DUMU PN]
13) [im-ḫur]
iii 1) 1 Mu-mu
2) 1 DINGIR-dan
3) DUMU We-tum
4) 1 I-bí-a
5) DUMU DINGIR-GÀR
6) 1 DINGIR-su-a-ḫa
7) DUMU Ma-ma-ḫi-ir
8) 1 SI.A-um

9) DUMU Rí-iṣ-DINGIR

10) ŠU.NIGÍN 5 AB+ÁŠ

11) [2]+2(GUR) ŠE SAG.GÁL

12) a-na Lá-a-im

13) 6(GUR) ŠE SAG.GÁL

14) PÙ.ŠA-^{d}IM

15) ⌈....⌉

L.E. 1) ⌈....⌉-⌈ga⌉?()

67. (Umm-el-Jīr 1932, 346)

Light reddish-brown. 103 × 78 × 17 mm. Two-column tablet. List of fourteen very large fields in fourteen locations with the names of their owners. The fields total 1,830 IKU. Plate XXIX.

i 1) 5(BUR'U) GÁN

2) in GIŠ.KIN.TI^{KI}

3) a-na Da-da ši NIN

4) 8(BUR) GÁN

5) in A?-ra()-tim$^{\langle KI\rangle}$

6) a-na X.DÙ.DÙ ()

7) 2(BUR) 6(IKU) GÁN

8) in A-ra-ga-zu^{KI}

9) a-na Ì-za-za

10) SABRA.É

11) 1(BUR) 6(IKU) GÁN

12) in A-zu$^{K[I]}$

ii 1) a-na I-nin-DINGIR

2) DUMU A-ši-a-lí

3) 12(IKU) GÁN

4) in Ti-me^{KI}

5) a-na PÙ.ŠA-ḪAL([sign])

6) 1(BUR) 6(IKU) GÁN

7) KÁ Kiš [....]-pù-[...].

8) a-na Su$_{4}$-ma-⌈za⌉-ba ⌈NU⌉.BANDA

9) 1(BUR) [12?(IKU)] GÁN

10) in Su-ur-gal^{KI}

11) a-na I-da-DINGIR

12) 3(BUR) [GÁN]

13) in Ig-.[...^{KI}]

Rev. i 1) a-na PÙ.Š[A-....]

2) 1(BUR) ⌈6?(IKU)⌉ [GÁN]

3) in A-tu-⌈a?^{KI}⌉

4) a-na I-ku([sign])-tum

5) 1(BURʾU) 5(BUR) GÁN

6) in Ša-at-^{d}Tu-tu<KI>

7) a-na I-ti-[....]

8) SABRA.⌈É⌉

9) 1(BUR) ⌈6?(IKU)⌉ GÁN

10) i[n ...].-tu^{KI}

11) [a-na] SIMUG

12) [1?(BUR) 12?(IKU) GÁN]

13) [in ....]-lum^{KI}

ii 1) a-na Be-lí-a-mi

2) ARÁD Sa-tu-DINGIR

3) 2(BUR) GÁN

4) in E-dar-ri^{KI}

5) a-na Šu-ì-lí-su

6) DUMU La-e-pum

7) 1(BUR'U) 2(BUR) GÁN

8) KÁ Me-šum

9) a-na Be-lí-GÚ

10) SABRA

(double line)

11) ŠU.NIGÍN 1(ŠÁR) 4(BUR'U) 1(BUR) 6+⌈6⌉(IKU) GÁN

12) DINGIR-⌈su⌉-a-ḫ[a]

13) S[ABRA.É]?

68. (Umm-el-Jīr 1932, 347)

Light reddish-brown. 85 × 85 × 20 mm. Three-column tablet. Reverse uninscribed. Memo about small amounts of barley for the feeding of the household. Plate XXX.

i 1) 10(SILÀ) ŠE Da-da

2) 10(SILÀ) Ur-maḫ?

3) 10(SILÀ) I-la-ag-nu-id

4) [10(SILÀ) É?-a?-d]an

5) [10(SILÀ) DI]NGIR-na-zi-ir

6) [10(SILÀ) ...].-da?-ad?

7) ⌈10(SILÀ)⌉ U-da

8) 10(SILÀ) DINGIR-[....]

9) ⌈10(SILÀ)⌉ .[...]

10) [35(SILÀ)? ....]

ii 1) 40(SILÀ) a-na ANŠE.BAR.AN

2) šu-ut si-⌈ip-rí⌉?

3) 1(PI)? Ú-da-ad-ba-lí-il

4) 10(SILÀ) Mim(SAL)-ma-tum

5) 10(SILÀ) Ḫa-nu-nu

6) 10(SILÀ) ME-^{d}Nin-SAR

7) 10(SILÀ) Si-wa-⌈....⌉

8) 10(SILÀ) Pù-pù

9) 10(SILÀ) Šu-ì-lí-su

10) [1(PI)]? 30(SILÀ)? a-na mu-[n]a?-ki-im

iii 1) [20]?+20(SILÀ) ⌈a-na⌉ NINDA.MU.RA

2) 2(PI) Me-iḫ-r[í-^{d}]IM

3) 1(GUR) ŠE SAG.GÁL (no PN!)

4) 10(SILÀ) Šu-ì-lí-su

5) 2(PI) LÁ 5 SILÀ ŠE

6) ŠE.KÚ [illegible]

(double line)

7) ŠU.NIGÍN 3(GUR) 1?(PI) ŠE.KÚ É

Rev. (uninscribed)

69. (Umm-el-Jīr 1932, 348)

Light reddish-brown. 87 × 65 × 20 mm. Left side of an at least three-column tablet. Obverse flat, reverse flaked off. Account of different commodities. Cf. note on the parallel text Umm-el-Jīr 1932, 527. Plate XXXI.

(beginning destroyed, traces of a sign)

i 1') 6(IKU) GÁN

2') [1]+1 MU

3') ŠÁM-ma-at

4') Ù-ì-lí

5') Gi-šum
6') PA.TE.SI
7') it-ba-al
8') 1 ŠAḪ.ŠE
9') 2(BUR) 12(IKU) GÁN
10') ŠÁM-ma-at
11') Ù-ì-lí
12') 2 MU
13') AB+⌈ÁŠ⌉-um
14') i[t-ba-a]l

ii (beginning destroyed)
1') 1 [....]
2') 1 AN[ŠE ....]
3') 1 ANŠ[E].B[AR?.AN]
4') 1 SAL.ANŠE [....]
5') 40 [UDU]? (a small sign)
6') 8 ŠE GUR
7') Gi-nu-mu-bí DUB.SAR
8') Bil$_{x}$(GIŠ.BÍL)-lum-TUR^{KI}

iii (beginning destroyed)
1') DI[NGIR ....]
2') 1(BUR) 6(IKU) [GÁN]
3') IG[I ....]
4') [....]

Rev. (destroyed)

70. (Umm-el-Jīr 1932, 349)

Light reddish-brown. 48 × 32 × 15 mm. Receipt of small amounts of barley by four persons from two persons. Plate XXVII.

1) 2(GUR) ŠE SAG.GÁL

2) I-mi-É-a

3) im-ḫur

4) 3(GUR) I-mi-[DINGIR]? (only one sign missing)

5) im-ḫur

6) 6(GUR) ŠE SAG.GÁL

7) Ì-lí-a-ḫi

Rev. 8) AB+ÁŠ.URU[KI]

9) im-ḫur

10) 1(GUR) ŠE SAG.GÁL

11) É-a-rí-zi MIN?(⩸)

12) ŠU.NIGÍN 12 ŠE SAG.GÁL

13) ŠE Iš-má-Eš$_4$-dar

14) Be-lí-lí

15) i-ti-⌈na⌉

71. (Umm-el-Jīr 1932, 350)

Light brown. 43 × 29 × 12 mm. Delivery of large amounts of barley by two persons. Plate XXVIII.

1) [x(GUR) ŠE SAG]

2) E-la-an

3) MAR.TU

4) ub-lam

5) 20(GUR) ŠE SAG

6) [Ku?-r]u-DINGIR [DUMU] SI.A-um

Rev. 7) ub-lam

8) 10(GUR) ŠE SAG

9) Sa-tu-tu
10) PAB.PAB
11) ub-lam

72. (Umm-el-Jīr 1932, 351)

Reddish-brown. 48 × 32 × 14 mm. Receipt of barley by one man as price of his son, and receipt of barley by one woman as price of a field. Plate XXX.

1) [x KUG.BABBAR] GÍN
2) [x(GUR)] ŠE SAG.GÁL
3) [É]-da-mu
4) im-ḫur
5) ŠÁM DUMU-su
6) A-li-a-ḫu

Rev. 7) 4(GUR) ŠE SAG.GÁL
8) Gu-ba-tum
9) a-na ŠÁM GÁN
10) dam-ḫur

73. (Umm-el-Jīr 1932, 352)

Reddish-brown. 55 × 38 × 16 mm. Account of different commodities and implements. Plate XXXI.

1) 2+[x(GUR) ŠE]?.BAR_x.BAR_x(UD.UD)
2) 1(PI) GÚ.GÚ.GAL.GAL
3) 1(PI) BAPPIR
4) 2(PI) $MUNU_x$
5) 20(erasure) ^{GI}zi-na-tum (more probable than zi-zi-na-tum)
6) 5 šu-li-pum

7) 4 GIŠ.PÙ.PÙ

8) 2 GIŠ.KUM

Rev. (uninscribed)

(unfinished)

74. (Umm-el-Jīr 1932, 353)

Light brown. 60 × 43 × 17 mm. Issue on loan of small amounts of barley by seven persons. Text similar to Umm-el-Jīr 1932, 356. Plate XXXI.

1) 5(GUR) ŠE SAG.GÁL

2) Be-lí-BARAG

3) im-ḫur

4) 2(GUR) 2(PI) ŠE SAG.GÁL

5) Be-lí-ba-ni

6) 6(GUR) ŠE SAG.GÁL

7) Ta-ta

8) 2(PI) I-ti-É-a

9) 2(PI) A-mur-ru-um

10) 2(PI) Me-iḫ-ru-um

Rev. 11) 2(PI) Me-it-lik-um

12) ḫ[u-b]u-lum

13) [ŠU.NIGÍN 12]+3(GUR) 1+[1](PI) ŠE SAG.GÁL

14) in Ki?-[x-n]im

15) .[...]

16) IGI DUMU.SAL ⌈É⌉?-[me]?-me

17) ⌈È⌉

18) ḫu-bu-[li]m

75. (Umm-el-Jīr 1932, 354)

Very light brown. 50 × 35 × 15 mm. Obverse flat, covered by a seal impression showing a man fighting a goat (or a bull?), with a lion behind; reverse (with inscription) round. Letter of Zuzu to Puzuzu concerning bronze. Cf. Umm-el-Jīr 1932, 360. Plate XXXII.

Rev. 1) [en]-ma
2) [Zu]-zu
3) a-na Pù-su-su (sic)
4) [i]š-dè
5) [Šu-ì⌉-lí-su
6) [x]+3 GÍN ⌈UD.BAR⌉.KA(wr. SAG)
7) li-il-ga
L.E. 8) [a-na PN]
9) [l]i-ti-in

76. (Umm-el-Jīr 1932, 355)

Reddish-brown. 47 × 35 × 18 mm. Issue of sixty-one goats. Plate XXXII.

1) 61 ÚZ
2) I-lul-DINGIR
3) SIPA
4) ⌈È⌉
Rev. 5) [i]n? MU.E?.A?(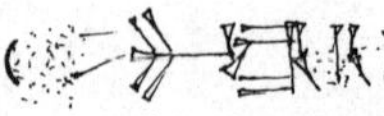)
6) LUGAL in É?-mar?(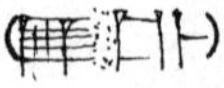)-nu-um
7) i-li-ga-am

77. (Umm-el-Jīr 1932, 356)

Reddish-brown. 41 × 30 × 18 mm. Issue on loan of

small amounts of barley by two persons. Text similar to Umm-el-Jīr 1932, 353. Plate XXXII.

1) 3?(PI) 20(SILÀ) <ŠE> M[u-x]-sa-[x]
2) 2(PI) 20(SILÀ) ŠE.K⌈Ú⌉
3) Aḫ-rí-um
4) 4(GUR) 3(PI) ŠE SAG.GÁL
5) Ba-ni-um
Rev. 6) ŠE ḫu-bu-lim
7) Be-lí-BARAG
8) È

78. (Umm-el-Jīr 1932, 357)

Light brown. 40 × 34 × 13 mm. Receipt on loan of large amount of barley by one person. Plate XXXIII.

1) 3(GUR) 2(PI) ŠE SAG.GÁL
2) Ur-kisal
3) im-ḫur
4) [ḫ]u-[b]u-lum
(rest uninscribed)

79. (Umm-el-Jīr 1932, 358)

Reddish-brown. 42 × 28 × 16 mm. Account of barley. Plate XXXIII.

1) 2(GUR) ŠE SAG.GÁL
2) Pù-a
3) 1(GUR) ŠE SAG.GÁL
4) Ú-KA-li
5) ḫu-bu-tum
6) 3(PI) 40(SILÀ) ŠE šu UD 1(\ )

7) 3(PI) ŠE

Rev. 8) šu UD 2()

9) 3(PI) <ŠE> šu UD 3()

10) 30(SILÀ) <ŠE> Pù-pù

11) SILÀ.ŠU.DU$_8$ a-na

12) Gú-da-im^{KI}

13) ub-AN

80. (Umm-el-Jīr 1932, 359)

Reddish-brown. 52 × 35 × 13 mm. Delivery of barley by four persons. Plate XXXIII.

1) 1(GUR) 2(PI) ŠE SAG

2) A-ḫi-da-áb(wr. ḪI)

3) DUB.SAR

4) 5(GUR) ŠE SAG

5) ARÁD-É-a

6) ub-lam

7) 3+[x](GUR) ŠE SAG

8) [P]ù-p[ù]

9) [u]b-l[am]

Rev. 10) [x(GUR)] ŠE SAG

11) [Ì?-t]um-ì-lum

12) ub-lam

81. (Umm-el-Jīr 1932, 360)

Reddish-brown. 35 × 30 × 13 mm. Letter of Zuzu to Šaṭpum concerning barley. Cf. Umm-el-Jīr 1932, 354. Plate XXXIII.

1) en-ma

2) Zu-zu

3) a-na Ša-at-pum

4) 1 ŠE GUR

5) a-na Šu-ì-lí-su

6) li-ti-in! (wr. clearly SAR = [sign] ; cf. 1932, 354:9)

Rev. (uninscribed)

82. (Umm-el-Jīr 1932, 361)

Reddish-brown. 33 × 27 × 12 mm. Receipt of barley as price of a house. Plate XXXIV.

1) 4(GUR) ŠE SAG.GÁL

2) KUG.BABBAR 2 1/2(DD [sign]) GÍN

3) ŠÁM É DINGIR-a-zu?([sign])

Rev. 4) Pù-pù

5) AB+ÁŠ.URU^{KI}

6) íl-ga

83. (Umm-el-Jīr 1932, 362)

Reddish-brown. 28 × 25 × 10 mm. Since both sides of the tablet are round, there is no way to distinguish the obverse from the reverse. In spite of the open space after line 3, which could mark the end of the text, we take the side with <u>en-ma</u> as the obverse. All signs perfectly written. Letter from Šūma-ṣaba' to Šuli'um concerning the watering of a field. Plate XXXIV.

1) en-ma

2) Su_4-ma-za-ba

3) a-na Su-NI-um

(space)

Rev. 4) a e-ni-im

5) GÁN

6) ša KÁ Kiš bi-mu-ut

7) ni-ti-ku

8) li-iš-ki-ù

84. (Umm-el-Jīr 1932, 363)

Reddish-brown. 35 × 25 × 12 mm. Receipt of silver, sheep, and barley by one man and his mother. Plate XXXIV.

1) ⌈KUG.BABBAR⌉ 3 1/2 GÍN.TUR

2) 1 UDU

3) 1(GUR) ŠE SAG

4) I-wi-ir-mu-bí

Rev. 5) DUMU É-a-dan

6) ME-^{d}Nin-su-AN

7) AMA-su

8) im-ḫu-ra

85. (Umm-el-Jīr 1932, 364)

Reddish-brown. 42 × 33 × 15 mm. Issue of a very large amount of barley to be used for bread of the household. Text unfinished. Plate XXXV.

1) 180+30+8(GUR) ŠE SAG

2) È

3) NINDA É

(rest uninscribed)

86. (Umm-el-Jīr 1932, 365)

Reddish-brown. 33 × 31 × 10 mm. Both sides roundish. Memo concerning large amount of silver borrowed by one person. Cf. Umm-el-Jīr 1932, 367. Plate XXXV.

1) 15 GÍN 1 MA.NA.TUR KUG.BABBAR

2) iš-dè

3) Be-lí-lí

Rev. 4) i-⌈ba⌉-šè

87. (Umm-el-Jīr 1932, 366)

Reddish-brown. 40 × 30 × 16 mm. Account of barley. Plate XXXV.

1) [x(GUR)] ⌈ŠE SAG⌉.GÁL

2) [i]n ti-im-ti

3) Gal-pum

4) 75(GUR) ŠE SAG.GÁL

5) Bur-zum

Rev. 6) 150(GUR) ŠE SAG.GÁL

7) KA-mu-um

8) MU.⌈DU⌉

(rest almost destroyed; probably nothing missing)

88. (Umm-el-Jīr 1932, 367)

Reddish-brown. 40 × 38 × 13 mm. Receipt of silver, and issue of barley. Cf. Umm-el-Jīr 1932, 365. Plate XXXVI.

1) 16 1/2 GÍN KUG.BABBAR

2) Be-lí-lí

3) AGRIG

4) im-ḫur

Rev. 5) 240 ⌈LÁ⌉ 10(GUR) ŠE GUR A-ga-dè^{KI}

6) È.A ŠE LIBIR

89. (Umm-el-Jīr 1932, 368)

Light brown. Bulky form. 48 × 50 × 18 mm. Possibly a school exercise. Plate XXXVI.

1) 2(GUR) 2(PI) a-na

2) KA-Lu-lu

3) ḪA.GUNU(crossed out)

4) X() PISAN.BE.BE

Rev. (uninscribed)

90. (Umm-el-Jīr 1932, 369)

Light brown. 37 × 35 × 16 mm. Roundish tablet. Probably a school exercise. Signs crossed out. Plate XXXVI.

1) 7(GUR) 2(PI) ŠE GUR

2) Íl-su(d)-a-ḫa

(rest uninscribed)

91. (Umm-el-Jīr 1932, 370)

Light reddish-brown. 67 × 65 × 17 mm. Circular (not four-sided) tablet. Obverse flat, reverse rounded. Writing on the reverse is oriented sideways in relation to the obverse. School exercise. Plate XXXVII.

1) Nu(wr.)-nu(wr.) (erasure)

2) Lugal-níg-lu-lu-a

3) du-ub-ḫa (erasure)
4) in A-ku-zum[KI]
5) [G]I? ZU ⌈X⌉

Rev. (space)

1) in La-lu-rí[KI]
2) la-ma-na-am
3) Ku-bí-GI
4) en-ma
5) ⌈A⌉-mur-DINGIR
6) ⌈a⌉-na

(space)

92. (Umm-el-Jīr 1932, 372a)

Five fragments, all Sargonic, not related. Largest fragment: Light brown. 40 × 40 × 11 mm. Obverse flat, reverse flaked off. Account of rations? of barley? Plate XXXVI.

1) 30(SILÀ) Pù-su-su (sic)
2) 30(SILÀ) PÙ.ŠA-su-ni
3) 30(SILÀ) DINGIR-ba-ni
4) 30(SILÀ) Ma-la-s[u]?
5) 30(SILÀ) Šu-Ma-[ma]
6) 30(SILÀ) PÙ.Š[A-....]

(rest destroyed)

Rev. (destroyed)

93. (Umm-el-Jīr 1932, 372b)

Light brown. 23 × 31 × 5 mm. A very small fragment. Reverse flaked off. Account of barley. Plate XXXVII.

(beginning destroyed)

1') 40 ŠE GUR.SAG.GÁL

(rest destroyed)

94. (Umm-el-Jīr 1932, 372c)

Light reddish-brown. 18 × 14 × 3 mm. A very small fragment. Reverse flaked off. Contents undefinable. Plate XXXVII.

(beginning destroyed)

1') 1 GIŠ [....] ŠÀ .[...]

(rest destroyed)

95. (Umm-el-Jīr 1932, 372d)

Light brown. 28 × 20 × 18 mm. A small fragment. Account of barley? Plate XXXVIII.

(beginning destroyed)

1') 1(PI) .[...]

2') 2(PI) 30(SILÀ) A-.[...]

3') 20(SILÀ) [....]

4') 40(SILÀ) [....]

5') 20(SILÀ)? [....]

Rev. 6') 1(PI) Ú-lu-[....] .[...]

7') 20(SILÀ) A-[....]

(rest destroyed)

96. (Umm-el-Jīr 1932, 372e)

Light brown. Worthless fragment. Reverse flaked off. Only BÍ visible. Plate XXXVII.

97. (Umm-el-Jīr? 1932, 402)

Reddish-brown. 67 × 40 × 16 mm. Reverse flaked off. Distribution of barley for various purposes. Plate XXXVII.

1) [x]+1(GUR) 2(PI) 50(SILÀ) ŠE GUR
2) [I]-bí-su(sic)
3) 10(GUR)+[x ŠE G]UR LÚ.ŠIM
4) 3(GUR) 30(SILÀ) ŠE GUR MU
5) 2(GUR) ŠE GUR ANŠE.BAR.AN
6) 13(GUR) 4(PI) UDU.⸢ŠE⸣
7) 10 LÁ 1 GUR ŠAḪ.[ŠE]
8) [x] GUR NÍG. 
9) (space)
Rev. (destroyed)

98. (Umm-el-Jīr 1932, 413)

Light brown. 58 × 47 × 26 mm. Left and bottom sides destroyed. At least two columns. Account of barley. Plate XXXVIII.

i (destroyed but for part of one sign)
ii 1) Mug-da-an^{KI}
2) 3 [ŠE G]UR En-bu-[DINGIR]
3) 3(PI)+[x? ...].(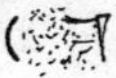)-mu-bí
4) [x]+20(SILÀ) Zu-zu-DINGIR
5) [x] ŠE GUR Ù-ù
6) [x] En-na-núm
7) [x]+30(SILÀ) PÙ.ŠA-ḪA[L]
(not DINGIR)

8) [x]+1(PI) Su-ku-kum

(double line)

9) [ŠU].NIGÍN 7 ŠE GUR

10) [X⌉-sal-la-[....]?

(rest destroyed)

Rev. i (beginning destroyed)

1') [...]. BÍ [....]?

2') [....] ⌈L⌉u-lu [....]?

3') [....] ⌈I⌉-lu[l?-DINGIR]?

4') [....] la [....]?

5') [....]

6') 1(PI) Su-ba-rí-um

7') 1(PI) 15 SILÀ Be-lí-sa-ki

(double line)

8') ŠU.NIGÍN 6+[3](GUR) 3(PI)
5 SILÀ ŠE GUR

9') [x] NU [x]?

ii (destroyed)

99. (Umm-el-Jīr 1932, 416)

Reddish-brown. 45 × 43 × 18 mm. Lower part of tablet destroyed. Account of fields with their measurements. Plate XXXVIII.

1) 30 LÁ 1 KUR 30 LÁ 2 [MAR.TU]

2) 25 U_5(ḪU.SI) 22 [MIR]

3) A.ŠÀ 6+1/2+1/4(IKU) GÁN ⌈X ŠE X⌉

4) 30 LÁ 2 U_5 30 [MIR]

5) [60]+2 KUR 40 [MAR.TU]

6) [A].ŠÀ 14+1/2+1/4(IKU) GÁN ŠE ⌈X⌉

7) [x]+2 MIR 20 LÁ [x U$_5$]

8) [x]+13 M[AR.TU x KUR]

(rest destroyed)

Rev. (beginning destroyed)

1') [....]

2') [....]

3') ⌈....⌉ É

4') 1(IKU) GÁN [....] ŠE ⌈X⌉

5') Ì-lí-dan

6') DA I-li-mu-bí

(end)

100. (Umm-el-Jīr 1932, 420)

Light reddish-brown. 43 × 37 × 14 mm. Account of wooden objects and sheep. Plate XXXIX.

1) 2 ^{GIŠ}ZI.NÀ(D) [MU]?.NI[GÍN]

(rest destroyed)

Rev. (beginning destroyed)

1') [a-na Mug-d]a-an$^{[\text{KI}]}$

2') [x] ⌈UDU⌉

3') [x ^{GIŠ}]ZI.NÀ(D) [M]U?.NIGÍN

4') I-da-ba-dar?(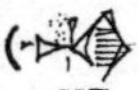)

5') a-na Mug-da-an^{KI}

6') ub-AN

101. (Umm-el-Jīr 1932, 527)

Light reddish-brown. 96 × 61 × 17 mm. At least two columns. Left side destroyed. Account of different commodities. Same color, same size of signs, and same contents as Umm-el-Jīr 1932, 348, but the two large fragments cannot be joined and must represent two different tablets. A parallel text is also to be found in BIN VIII 144. See PREFACE pp. xiv-xv. Plate XXXIX.

i' 1) [x] GURUŠ

2) [x] 1/3 ŠA.NA GÍN KUG.BABBAR

3) [x] GEMÉ

4) [x] GÍN KUG.BABBAR

5) [x] GEMÉ

6) [x ŠE G]UR

(rest destroyed)

ii' 1) 1 Gu-gu-š⌈a⌉

2) 2 MU

3) Lu-lu it-ru

4) KUG-su 1/3 ŠA.NA 4 GÍN KUG.BABBAR

5) ša MU 2.KAM.MA

6) Ù-ì-lí

7) ig-ri-su

8) i-ti-in

9) 22 ŠE GUR

10) in Mug-da-an^{KI}

11) 15 ŠE GUR

12) 1(PI) ZÍD.ŠE

13) 1(PI) MUNU$_x$.GAZ

14) in Bil$_x$(GIŠ.BÍL)-lum-GAL^{KI}

15) [šu] ⌈Ù⌉-ì-lí

Rev. i 1) [Lu-l]u

2) [iš-l]u-ul

3) [x] GEMÉ

4) [x]+6 ŠE GUR

5) [x] ŠE GUR

6) [Be-lí]-ba-⌈ni⌉

7) [....]

8) [x]+5 ŠE GUR

(rest destroyed)

102. (Kish IM 23302)

Brown. 63 × 41 × 18 mm. Receipt of silver by several <u>bêlū</u> "lords." Cf. also Kish 1930, 152 end.

1) [x] GÍN [KUG.BABBAR]

2) 1 I-g[u-núm]

3) 1 PÙ.ŠA-iš-⌈su⌉?( )

4) 1 Ì-lí-TAB.BA

5) ù DAM-zu

6) 1 Zu-zu

7) 1 ARAD?-DÙG?( )

8) [1] I-nin?-um?

9) [x] GÍN KUG.BABBAR

Lo.E. 9a) [....]?

Rev. 10) ⌈....⌉

11) u-bil$_x$(GIŠ.BIL)

12) 1 Pù-pù

13) 1 Pù-sa-šum

14) be-lu KUG.BABBAR

103. (Kish IM 23304)

Gray-brown. 63 × 40 × 18 mm. Bottom and right edge

of obverse destroyed. Distribution of barley to women.

1) 1(PI)(wr. ▽) DAM Be-lí-lí
2) 1(PI) DAM A-mur-u[m]
3) 1(PI) Da-mi-tum
4) 1(PI) Ia-ab?(⊏⊐)-zi-[tum]?
5) 1(PI) DAM Im-m⌈u-x]
6) 1(PI) [....]
(rest destroyed)

Rev. (beginning destroyed)
1') 1(PI) [....]
2') 1(PI) DAM [....]
3') 1(PI) ⌈DAM⌉ [....]
4') 1(PI) ^{d}K[A-....]
5') 1(PI) DAM Zi-lu-[lu]
6') 1(PI) DAM Ku-ru-DINGIR-(x)?

104. (Kish IM 23305)

Light brown. 42 × 32 × 17 mm. Issue of barley for various purposes.

1) [x(GUR) or x(PI)] 24 SILÀ ŠE
2) ŠÁM IZI.TUR
3) 40(SILÀ) ŠE KAŠ [nothing]?
4) 30(SILÀ) ŠE ar-sa-núm
5) [x]+10(SILÀ) ŠE BAR.AN.NIT[A]
6) [x(SILÀ) Š]E ZÍD.GU

Rev. 7) [....]
8) 30(SILÀ) ⌈a⌉-na ŠE.ḪAR KAŠ
9) 20(SILÀ) ŠE.⌈KA.GAR?⌉ ŠAḪ.Ú

10) 1(GUR) 1(PI) 20(SILÀ) ZA-.[...]
(space)
11) [MU]?.DU ŠE

105. (Ashmolean 1924, 655)

Reddish-brown. 65 × 48 × 17 mm. Linear numbers. Memo about the exchange of four fields owned by four individuals for oxen. Plate XL.

1) 5(IKU) GÁN
2) Lú-nigir
3) 4(IKU) Si-du(sic)
4) 6+6+1(IKU) GÁN
5) Lugal-èn(LI)-tar-sir
6) 6+3+1/2+1/4(IKU) Ur-^{d}En-ki
(double line)
7) ŠU.NIGÍN 18+12+1+1/2+1/4(IKU) GÁN
Rev. 8) Šeš-šeš ENGAR
9) a-na ŠÁM GUD

106. (Ashmolean 1924, 661)

Light brown. 92 × 48 × 16 mm. Record of fourteen orchards, with their date-palms, owners, and/or gardeners. Plate XLI.

1) 95 ^{GIŠ}GIŠIMMAR
2) ^{GIŠ}SAR Ur-barag
3) 23 ^{GIŠ}GIŠIMMAR
4) ^{GIŠ}SAR Lugal-iti-da
5) 60+⌈60⌉? ^{GIŠ}GIŠIMMAR
6) ^{GIŠ}SAR ^{d}En-líl

7) NI-si$_4$ NU.SAR

8) 40 LÁ 2 ^{GIŠ}GIŠIMMAR

9) ^{GIŠ}SAR Ur-pisan

10) 151 ^{GIŠ}GIŠIMMAR

11) ^{GIŠ}SAR Íd-šà

12) 44 ^{GIŠ}GIŠIMMAR

13) ^{GIŠ}SAR É-li-li

14) Ur-pisan NU.SAR

Rev. 15) 55 ^{GIŠ}GIŠIMMAR

16) Nam-maḫ-ni NU.SAR

17) 26 ^{GIŠ}GIŠIMMAR

18) ^{GIŠ}SAR SIG$_4$.KUR

19) 105 ^{GIŠ}GIŠIMMAR

20) Lum-ma NU.SAR

21) 62 ^{GIŠ}GIŠIMMAR

22) ^{GIŠ}SAR Lugal-lú

23) 50 ^{GIŠ}GIŠIMMAR

24) ^{GIŠ}[S]AR-maḫ

25) 76 ^{GIŠ}GIŠIMMAR

26) ^{GIŠ}SAR-kug

27) En-úr NU.SAR

28) 74 ^{GIŠ}GIŠIMMAR

29) ^{GIŠ}SAR-gíd-da

L.E. 30) 32 ^{GIŠ}GIŠIMMAR ^{GIŠ}SAR Du-du

40 GIŠ(wr. 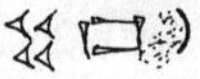)

(apparently unfinished)

107. (Ashmolean 1924, 662)

Light brown. 74 × 40 × 13 mm. Linear numbers. Record

of different kinds of flour assigned to five persons. The amount of 7 1/2 silà remaining from the sum in line 16 cannot be fitted anywhere, certainly not in line 1. Plate XL.

1) ⌈40⌉?(silà) [NI]NDA.ḪAR.RA sig_5
2) 50+3 silà NINDA.ḪAR.RA gin
3) 2(pi) zíd-še
4) Šu-Dur-al(sic)
5) 15 silà zíd-še
6) 6 silà zíd-gu
7) 1 silà NINDA.ḪAR.RA
8) 1 silà še ar-za-na
9) Gú-sil-lá MU
10) 3 silà NINDA.ḪAR.RA
11) 5 silà zíd-DUB.DUB
12) A-$ša_6$-$ša_6$
13) 6 silà zíd-še

Rev. 14) UŠ.KU-maḫ
15) 1 silà É-b[a?-s]um
(space)
16) še-bi 4(pi) 18 1/2 silà
17) A-$ša_6$-$ša_6$
18) A-ši-DINGIR.RA-šè
19) im-gin-na-a
20) zi-ga
21) Da-da

108. (Ashmolean 1924, 663)

Light brown. 66 × 43 × 13 mm. Distribution of barley,

silver, and sheep to five persons. 1 gur-maḫ = 300 silà; ŠÁM+2 = 120 še; igi-3-gál = 60 še. Plate XLII.

1) 30(GUR) LÁ 2(PI) 30(SILÀ)
ŠE GUR.MAḪ
2) 1 UDU
3) En-ZU.AB
4) 20(GUR) LÁ 3(PI) GUR
5) 4 1/2 GÍN 10 ŠE KUG.BABBAR
6) Lugal-iti-da DUB.SAR
7) IGI.3.GÁL 20 ŠE KUG
8) Ur-ša$_6$
9) ⌈LÚ⌉?(...).GIŠ.NI
Rev. 10) 1 GÍN ŠÁM+2 20 ŠE KUG
11) Lugal-iti-da SIPA
12) 1(GUR) 3(PI) 30(SILÀ) GUR
13) Lú-A+ḪA
14) ù Me-PA.GAN
(double line)
15) ŠU.NIGÍN 50(GUR) 3(PI) ŠE
GUR.MAḪ
16) ŠU.NIGÍN 6 GÍN ŠÁM+2 20 ŠE KUG
17) ŠU.NIGÍN 1 UDU
18) [....]? MU 3.KAM

109. (Ashmolean 1924, 664)

Light brown. 38 × 34 × 13 mm. Linear numbers. Delivery of BAPPIR to the É.ÙR. Plate XLI.

1) 120+20 LÁ 3 [BAPPI]R.SIG$_5$
2) A.RÁ 1.KAM

3) 180+21 BAPPIR

4) [A.R]Á 2.KAM

Rev. 5) a-na É.ÙR

6) è-ru-ub

110. (Ashmolean 1924, 680)

Reddish-brown. 62 × 46 × 17 mm. Inventory of an individual. Plate XLII.

1) 1 TÚG.BAR.TÚG

2) 1 TÚG.ŠU

3) 3 TÚG.NÍG.DÙN(=GÍN without GUNU).DÙ

4) 2 TÚG.BAR.TÚG BE (old)

5) 3 ma-na síg

6) 2 GI. síg

7) 2 TÚG.UŠUM

8) 5 gín an-na urudu

Rev. 9) 2 giš-rín

10) 1 TÚG.ŠÀ.GA.DÙ

(space)

11) níg-ga Ur-ša$_6$-kam

111. (Ashmolean 1924, 684)

Reddish-brown. 55 × 43 × 17 mm. Account of barley of two persons in Giršu. Plate XLIII.

1) 60+10 ŠE GUR.MAḪ

2) šu Lugal-ra

3) 60+5 <ŠE> GUR

4) šu Šeš-kal-la

(space)

5) in Gír-su^{KI}

Rev. (uninscribed)

112. (Ashmolean 1924, 689)

Reddish-brown. 48 × 45 × 13 mm. Linear numbers. All signs perfectly written. The measures of length in lines 1-2 may represent the four sides of a rectangle. Multiplying 216,240 GAR + 4 KÙŠ.NUMUN by 3,692 GAR + 10 KÙŠ.NUMUN we get about 800,000,000 GAR^2 = about 800,000,000 SAR = about 8,000,000 IKU = about 3,000,000 hectares = about 30,000 km^2. The measures of surface in line 4 have two very high measures unknown before: ŠÁR.LÍL and ŠÁR+U.GAL. Taking them as progressively rising numbers, we obtain altogether an area of about 500,000 IKU = about 200,000 hectares = 2,000 km^2, a number which does not correspond to the area as reconstructed from multiplying the length by the width of the sides of lines 1-2. The text yields immense areas and is ununderstandable to me. Plate XLIII.

1) 1×ŠÁR.GAL 240 GAR
   4 KÙŠ.NUMUN SÁ

(space)

2) 1×ŠÁR 92 GAR
   10 KÙŠ.NUMUN SÁ

3) Ur-^{d}KA.DI

Rev. 4) 7×ŠÁR.LÍL 4×ŠÁR+U.GAL
   7×ŠÁR 1×BUR+U 7×BUR 6+
   3 1/2 IKU 10 SAR

16 GÍN 2/3 ŠA

5) BA.PÀD

113. (Ashmolean 1924, 692)

Reddish-brown. 54 × 42 × 13 mm. Receipt of different kinds of flour by two persons. Plate XLIII.

1) 3(GUR) 2(PI) 30(SILÀ) ZÍD.ŠE
GUR.SI.SÁ

2) 45 SILÀ ZÍD.GU

3) 35 SILÀ ZÍD.KAL

4) 10(SILÀ) BAPPIR

5) 40(SILÀ) AR.ZA.NA

6) KI Gemé-TAR

7) [x] ZÍD.KAL

Rev. 8) [x ZÍD].GU

9) šu Da-da

10) Uru-ki

11) im-⌈ḫur⌉

For Nos. 114-116 see pp. xxviii-xxx.

INDICES OF PROPER NAMES

1. Personal Names

The personal names are arranged in the order of the Latin alphabet. The logograms occurring in the Akkadian names have not been transliterated into Akkadian but retained in their Sumerian form in harmony with the transliterations in the main part of this volume.

The following abbreviations for genealogical relationships are used in this list: s. for son, d. for daughter, gs. for grandson, f. for father, m. for mother, gf. for grandfather, br. for brother, sis. for sister, h. for husband, and w. for wife. The entry (f.n.) stands for a feminine personal name.

The first entries in the references are abbreviated in the following way:

27, ... to 31, ... stands for Kish 1927, ... to Kish 1931, ..., in the Ashmolean Museum (= Nos. 1-65).

32, ... stands for Umm-el-Jīr 1932, ..., in the Ashmolean Museum (= Nos. 66-101).

IM .... stands for Kish 1935, in the Iraq Museum (= Nos. 102-104).

24, ... stands for Sargonic texts of unknown origin, in the Ashmolean Museum (= Nos. 105-113).

A-[....], 32, 372d 2', 7'

Á-a-pum ⌈f. of⌉ Gu-ra-tum, 30, 177g 3

A-bí-DÙG, 30, 144 rev. ii 4

A-d[a]?, 30, 348b 4'

A-ḫi-da-áb(wr. ḪI) DUB.SAR, 32, 359:2

A-ḫu-DINGIR, 31, 122 iv 19

A-ḫu-DÙG, 31, 122 iv 18

A-ḫu-ḫu, 30, 146:4

[A]-ḫu-mu-bí f. of U-ba-ru-um, 30, 559d 6

A-ḫu-ni-si(g) f. of DINGIR-a-ḫa, 30, 177n 14

A-ku-DINGIR, 31, 143:26

  ⌈A⌉?-ku-DINGIR, 31, 143:13

A-li-a-ḫu UGULA, 30, 406 ii 4

  A-li-a-ḫu s. of [É]-da-mu, 32, 351:6

  A-li-a-ḫu f. of Šu-ì-lí-su, 30, 144 ii 4

A-li-li (f.n.), 31, 121 i 5, 11

  A-lí-lí UGULA, 30, 177g 6

A-ma-.[...] (f.n.), 31, 121 i 8

A-mur-DINGIR, 30, 138:5; 30, 145:12

  ⌈A⌉-mur-DINGIR, 32, 370 rev. 5

  A-mur-DINGIR DUB.SAR, 30, 144 rev. ii 14

  A-mur-D[INGIR]: ⌈Ì⌉-za-n[i]? šu A-mur-D[INGIR], 31, 136:6'

A-mur?-DÙG d. of Rí-iš-tum, 31, 121 ii 5

A-mur-ru-k[i?-m]a?-DINGIR, 31, 143:6

A-mur-ru-um, 32, 353:9

  A-mur-u[m], IM 23304:2

A-mur-^{d}UTU f. of U-ba-ru-um, 30, 144 ii 15

A-na-d[a]?-rí: ⌈Nu⌉?-ni-da šu A-na-d[a]?-rí, s. of É-a-DÙG, 30, 406 ii 8

A-ni-ni, see under A-li-li

Be-lí-ba-lik, 31, 122 i 13

Be-lí-ba-ni, 32, 353:5

  [Be-lí]-ba-⌈ni⌉, 32, 527 rev. 6

Be-lí-BÀD-rí (f.n.), 31, 121 i 7

Be-lí-BARAG, 32, 353:2: 32, 356:7

Be-lí-DÙG šu Gàr-tum SI[PA Á]B, 30, 406 rev. ii 16

Be-lí-^{d}EN.ZU, 30, 149:5

Be-lí-GÚ SABRA, 32, 346 rev. ii 9

Be-lí-lí, 32, 349:14; 32, 365:3; IM 23304:1

  Be-lí-lí AGRIG, 32, 367:2

Be-lí-sa-ki, 32, 413 rev. i 7'

Bí-bí, 30, 559b 2

Bí-la-lum, 30, 768:5

Bu-BALA, see under Pù-

[B]u?-du$_{8}$-um [f. of? ....]-NI, 30, 151:2

Bu-ga-núm, 31, 121 rev. i 7

  B[u]?-ga-núm, 31, 122 ii 11

[B]u?-ra-núm ⌈s. of⌉? Za-ab-tum, 30, 151:3

Bur-zum, 32, 366:5

  Bur-zum f. of Zi-ra, 31, 418:5

Da-ak(-x?)-mu-um, 31, 122 rev. i 19

Da-áš-má-tum (f.n.), 30, 768:3

Da-ba-ba, 32, 345 ii 10

  [D]a-ba-ba, 31, 143:12

Da-bí-bí, 30, 170c 3

Da-da, 24, 662:21; 24, 692:9; 30, 140:1; 32, 347 i 1

  Da-da ši (gen.) NIN, 32, 346 i 3

  Da-da: Da-kum šu Da-da, 31, 418:15

En-kug f. of Ì-lí-bi-la-ni, 30, 175i 5'

En-l[i]?, 31, 122 rev. i 15

En-na-DINGIR ⌈f. of⌉ I-lul-DINGIR, ARÁD-zu-ni, and Ìr-su-tum, 31, 134:3

En-na-na, 30, 559f 4

En-na-núm, 32, 413 ii 6

En-úr NU.SAR, 24, 661:27

En-ZU.AB, 24, 663:3

^{d}EN.ZU-al-su f. of Gu-lí-lí, 31, 418:12

^{d}EN.ZU-iš-da-<gal>: DINGIR-su-ra-bí šu ^{d}EN.ZU-iš-da-<gal>, 30, 406 rev. i 5

^{d}EN.ZU-ni-⌈sá⌉ (f.n.), 31, 121 i 6

Eš$_4$-[da]r-ba-luḫ, 30, 170c 2

Eš$_4$-dar-BÀD-rí m.? of Šu-ì-lí-su and? Pù-zu-zu, 31, 121 ii 11

Eš$_4$-dar-dan A.AZU, 30, 144 rev. ii 12

Eš$_4$-dar-É GEMÉ, 30, 145:11

Eš$_4$-dar-ni-sa f. of I-bí-bí, 30, 144 ii 6

Eš$_4$-dar-nu-id f. of Ì-lu-lu, 30, 139:2

Ga-áš-tum-BALA f. of É-da-mu, 30, 406 rev. i 8

Ga-la-ab-É-a, 30, 170b 4

Ga-li-l[i], 31, 133:18'

Ga-zu-a-lum, 30, 144 rev. ii 3

GAL?-[....], 31, 122 iv 9

Gal-pum, 31, 122 ii 8

  Gal-pum, 32, 366:3

  Gal-pum s. of Du-li-li, 31, 121 ii 14

GAL.ZU, 31, 122 i 16

GAL.ZU-DI.TAR, 30, 140:9

[G]àr-[t]um SIPA ÁB [f. of] Si-ir-ga-núm, 30, 406 ii 17

Gàr-tum: Be-lí-DÙG šu Gàr-tum SI[PA Á]B, 30, 406 rev. ii 17

Gàr-tum ZAG.ḪA: Ì-lí-a-ḫi šu Gàr-tum ZAG.ḪA, 30, 406 iii 7

Gemé-tar, 24, 692:6

Gi-nu-mu-bí DUB.SAR, 32, 348 ii 7'

Gi-šum s. of Ì-lí-dan, 30, 559d 3

Gi-šum PA.TE.SI, 32, 348 i 5

GIGIR-la (f.n.), 31, 121 i 17

Gu-ba-tum (f.n.), 32, 351:8

Gu-gu-š⌈a⌉, 32, 527 ii 1

Gu-lí-lí d. of ᵈEN.ZU-al-su, 31, 418:11

Gu-lí-zu[m], br. of PÙ.ŠA-.[...], s. of ⌈I-ku?-ᵈ?KA⌉, 30, 144 rev. i 4

Gu-nu-núm šu La-mu-um LÚ.SIRIS, 30, 406 i 6

Gu-nu-tum f. of I-da-DINGIR, 30, 406 iii 2

Gu-ra-tum ⌈s. of⌉ Á-a-pum, 30, 177g 2

Gú-sil-lá MU, 24, 662:9

Gur-bu-bu, 30, 144 ii 7

[G]ur-bu-bu, 31, 130 ii 2'

[Gur-b]u?-bu, 30, 170d 14

Ḫ⌈a⌉-[....], 30, 142:2

Ḫa-nu-nu, 32, 347 ii 5

Ḫa-r[a-x], 31, 122 iii 10

ᵈ⌈Ḫa⌉?-rí-im-be-lí MAŠKIM, 30, 170c 6

[Ḫ]u?-ḫ[u?-....], 30, 767:11

Ḫu-zu-us-DINGIR ARÁD LUGAL, 30, 406 rev. ii 7

⌈I⌉?-ba-LUM, 30, 152:8

I-bi-um, 30, 140:11

I-bí-a s. of DINGIR-GÀR, 32, 345 rev. iii 4

I-bí-bí s. of Eš$_4$-dar-ni-sa, 30, 144 ii 5

I-bí-DINGIR UGULA, 30, 406 rev. i 6

I-bí-^{d}Nanše f. of Su-ru-uš-GI, 30, 177n 8

[I]-bí-su, 32, 402:2

[I]-bí-u[m], 31, 133:8'

I-bí-^{d}Za-ba$_4$-ba$_4$ s. of Pù-ni-a, 30, 406 i 1

I-bí-zu, 31, 122 i 8

I-da-ba-dar?, 32, 420 rev. 4'

I-da-DINGIR, 32, 346 ii 11

[I]-da-DINGIR, 31, 122 i 20

I-da-DINGIR UGULA, 30, 146:2

I-da-DINGIR s. of Gu-nu-tum, 30, 406 iii 1

I-da-^{d}EN.ZU, 30, 767:6

I-g[u-núm], IM 23302:2

I-ku-^{d}Ìr-ra, 31, 122 ii 5

⌈I-ku?-$^{d?}$KA⌉ f. of Gu-lí-z[um] and PÙ.ŠA-.[...], 30, 144 rev. i 6

I-ku-tum, 32, 346 rev. i 4

I-kul-um br. of Su-um-LUM, s. of Ì-lí-sa-liq, 30, 559a 1

I-la-ag-nu-id, see Ì-la-ag-nu-id

I-li-mu-bí, 32, 416 rev. 6'

I-lí-lí, see Ì-lí-lí

I-lul-DINGIR br. of ARÁD-zu-ni and Ìr-su-tum, ⌈s. of⌉ En-na-DINGIR, 31, 134:8

I-ti-É-a, 32, 353:8

I-ti-ti, 30, 144 ii 18; 31, 122 iv 17

  [I?-t]i-ti, 30, 347b rev. i 4

  I-ti-ti s. of Im$_x$(DU)-da-lik, 30, 177n 9

I-tu-[tu]?, 31, 144a rev. 1'

I-wi-ir-mu-bí s. of É-a-dan and ME-^{d}Nin-su-AN (f.n.), 32, 363:4

  ⌈I⌉-wi-ir-mu-bí br. of DINGIR-la-ag-nu-id and Šu-ì-lí-su, s. of É-a-dan, 32, 345 rev. i 6

Ì-la-ag-nu-id, 30, 148:8; 30, 149:7

  DINGIR-ag-nu-id s. of É-a-dan, 32, 345 iii 6

  DINGIR-nu-id (s. of É-a-dan), 32, 345 rev. i 2

  DINGIR-la-ag-nu-id br. of ⌈I⌉-wi-ir-mu-bí and Šu-ì-lí-su, s. of ⌈É⌉-a-da[n], 32, 345 rev. i 7

  I-la-ag-nu-id s. of É?-a?-dan, 32, 347 i 3

  Ì-la-ag-nu-id s. of Ub-da, 30, 177n 5

  Ì-la-ag-nu-id ⌈f. of⌉ DINGIR-a-zu, 30, 177g 5

Ì-la-nu-id f. of É-da-mu, 30, 139:7; 30, 144 rev. i 10

Ì-la-la, 30, 148:9; 30, 175c 2'; 31, 143:15

  ⌈Ì⌉-la-la UGULA, 30, 406 rev. ii 15

⌈Ì⌉-lí-a-bí d. of DINGIR-ra-bí ⌈s. of⌉ [....-LU]GAL?, 30, 559e 3

Ì-lí-a-ḫi, 31, 122 i 14

  Ì-lí-a-ḫi AB+ÁŠ.URU^{KI}, 32, 349:7

  [Ì-l]í?-a-ḫi: [....-u]m [s. of? It-be]?-la-ba [ši? Ì-l]í?-a-ḫi, 30, 406 i 12

  Ì-lí-a-ḫi šu Gàr-tum ZAG.ḪA, 30, 406 iii 6

Ì-lí-BALA, 31, 143:22

Ì-lí-be-lí AB+ÁŠ: Ku-ru-ub-Ì-la-ag šu Ì-lí-be-lí

AB+ÁŠ, 30, 406 ii 6

Ì-lí-bi-la-ni s. of En-kug, 30, 175i 4'

Ì-lí-BÍ, 32, 345 i 7

⌈Ì⌉-lí-BÍ, 30, 152:4

Ì-lí-BÍ s. of Ì-lu-lu, 30, 152:14

Ì-lí-dan, 30, 140:2; 30, 767:5; 31:122 ii 2; 32, 416 rev. 5'

Ì-lí-dan UGULA, 30, 144 i 14; 30, 170a 2

Ì-lí-dan ⌈f. of⌉? DINGIR-dan, 30, 144 i 5

Ì-lí-dan f. of Gi-šum, 30, 559d 4

Ì-lí-du-gul-ti, 30, 139:7

[Ì-lí-d]u-gul-ti, 30, 170c 4

Ì-lí-en-nu, 31, 122 i 12

Ì-lí-GAL SUKKAL, 30, 146:5

Ì-lí-iš-da-gal, 27, 1:3; 30, 170g 6

[Ì]-lí-iš-da-gal, 30, 152:10

Ì-lí-iš-da-gal s. of DINGIR-su-dan, 30, 559c rev. 2'

Ì-lí-lí (f.n.), 31, 121 i 15

⌈I⌉-lí-lí, 30, 140:8

I-lí-[lí] UGULA, 30, 144 rev. i 15

I-lí-lí (UGULA), 30, 170a 8

I-lí-lí UGULA, 30, 175b 2

I-lí-lí [UGULA], 30, 175c 1'

Ì-lí-lí f. of DINGIR-su-a-ḫa, 30, 144 i 16

[Ì]-lí-sa-liq, 31, 122 iv 15

Ì-lí-sa-liq f. of I-kul-um and Su-um-LUM, 30, 559a 3, 7

[Ì-l]í?-SIPA, 31, 133:12'

Ì-lí-TAB.BA, IM 23302:4

DINGIR-ga-lí s. of Ku-⌈....⌉, 30, 559a 4

DINGIR-ga-lí ⌈f. of⌉ Um-mi-Eš$_4$-dar, 30, 144 i 8

DINGIR-GAL.ZU X, 30, 148:7

DINGIR-GÀR, 30, 559f 1

DINGIR-GÀR X, 30, 148:5

DINGIR-GÀR f. of I-bí-a, 32, 345 rev. iii 5

DINGIR-GÀR f. of Íl-e-um, 30, 406 rev. i 10

DINGIR-GÀR [f. of] Šu-^{d}En-líl, 30, 177n 16

DINGIR-GÚ, 30, 138:13; 31, 122 i 15

DINGIR-GÚ MAŠKIM, 30, 170e 11

DINGIR-GÚ NAR, 30, 170f 8

DINGIR-GÚ NAR MAŠKIM, 30, 170d 8

DINGIR-la-ag-nu-id, see Ì-la-ag-nu-id

DINGIR-mu-[da], 30, 177h rev. 1'; 31, 143:23

[DINGIR]-mu-da, 31, 143:17

DINGIR-mu-da UGULA, 30, 406 iii 5

[DI]NGIR-na-zi-ir, 32, 347 i 5

DINGIR-nu-id, see Ì-la-ag-nu-id

DINGIR-ra-bí ⌈s. of⌉ [....-LU]GAL?, f. of ⌈Ì⌉-lí-a-bí, 30, 559e 4

DINGIR-SIPA UGULA, 30, 406 i 3

DINGIR-su-a-ḫa, 30, 170c 14; 30, 175c 4'

[DI]NGIR-su-a-ḫa, 30, 152:6

DINGIR-⌈su⌉-a-ḫ[a] S[ABRA.É]?, 32, 346 rev. ii 12

DINGIR-su-a-ḫa s. of Ì-lí-lí, 30, 144 i 15

DINGIR-su-a-ḫa s. of Ma-ma-ḫi-ir, 32, 345 rev. iii 6

DINGIR-su-dan, 30, 140:22

DINGIR-su-dan s. of Ì-lu-lu, 30, 559d 1

DINGIR-su-dan s. of I-mi-DINGIR, 31, 418:7, 32

Im-m⌈u-x], IM 23304:5

^{d}IM-[....] s. of Rí-ig-mu-[um], 30, 144 rev. i 13

^{d}IM-sar, 30, 170d 4

^{d}IM-sar f. of [Ku?-r]u-UR.SAG, 30, 177n 2

Im$_{x}$(DU)-da-lik, 30, 150:3; 31, 122 iv 16

[Im$_{x}$(DU)-d]a?-lik, 30, 170d 13

Im$_{x}$(DU)-da-lik X, 30, 148:1

Im$_{x}$(DU)-da-lik f. of I-ti-ti, 30, 177n 10

Im$_{x}$(DU)-da-lik: [....]-DINGIR šu Im$_{x}$(DU)-da-lik DUMU ši A-tu-tu, 30, 406 rev. ii 3

Ip-ḫur-⌈....⌉, 31, 122 ii 4

Ip-kum, 30, 140:15; 30, 146:3

Ip-kum UGULA, 30, 148:4

Ip-kum (UGULA), 30, 170a 4

Ip-šum, 30, 140:12

Ip-šu[m] UGULA, 30, 144 ii 13

Ip-šum (UGULA), 30, 170a 11

Ip-šum UGULA, 30, 177g 1

Ir-[....], 31, 122 iii 12

Ìr-e-pum, 30, 768:4

Ìr-e-pum s. of I-sar-ni-si(g)-sa-am, 30, 144 i 12

⌈Ìr⌉-na-⌈....⌉-núm, 30, 406 rev. i 11

Ìr-su-tu-um, 32, 345 ii 8

Ìr-su-tum br. of ARÁD-zu-ni and I-lul-DINGIR, ⌈s. of⌉ En-na-DINGIR, 31, 134:7

[Ì]r-su-t[um]?, 31, 136:9'

Ìr-šum, 30, 349b 2

Iš-dup-DINGIR, 30, 144 rev. ii 8

⌈Iš⌉-dup-pum, 31, 122 ii 9

Iš$_x$(LAM+KUR)-e-si-na-at, 30, 175c 6'

Iš$_x$([L]AM+KUR)-gi-u[m], 31, 122 iii 15

Iš-ku-DINGIR, 30, 559c 5'

Iš-lul-DINGIR s. of DINGIR-[....], 30, 144 rev. i 11

Iš-má-^{d}[....], 31, 121 iii 3

Iš-má-a-ni f. of La-gi-pum, 30, 150:2

[I]š-má-DINGIR, 30, 177g 9

Iš-má-^{d}EN.ZU, 30, 142:9; 30, 170b 5

Iš-má-Eš$_4$-dar, 32, 349:13

  Iš?-má-<Eš$_4$>-dar?, 31, 143:18

  [Iš?-má]?-Eš$_4$-dar, 31, 143:11

Iš-má-KÁR, 30, 140:4, 21

  Iš-m[á-K]ÁR (UGULA), 30, 170a 3

  [Iš]-má-KÁR [s. of] DINGIR-su-dan, 30, 144 i 2

  Iš-má-KÁR f. of DINGIR-su-dan, 30, 177n 4

It-be-⌈ba⌉-la, 31, 122 ii 6

It-be-la-ba, 30, 170d 10

  It-be-la-ba f. of PÙ.ŠA-^{d}Nu-ni and PÙ.ŠA-^{d}Za-ba$_4$-ba$_4$, 30, 144 i 11

  [It-be]?-la-ba [f. of? ....-u]m [ši? Ì-l]í?-a-ḫi, 30, 406 i 13

^{d}K⌈A-....], 31, 122v 14

  ^{d}K[A-....] (f.n.), IM 23304 rev. 4'

^{d}KA-Me-ir f. of ⌈Z⌉a-na-d⌈a⌉, 32, 345 ii 3

KA-lu-lu, 32, 368:2

KA-mu-um, 32, 366:7

Ki-[....], 30, 144 rev. i 22

Ki-.[...], 31, 122 iv 22

Ki-bí-^{d}EN.ZU, 27, 1:2

Ki-bu-tum, 30, 170b 3

Ki-im-m[a-x] f. of Na-bí-[um], 30, 144 ii 12

Ku-⸢....⸣ f. of DINGIR-ga-lí, 30, 559a 5

Ku-bí-GI, 32, 370 rev. 3

Ku-ku, 30, 140:10

  Ku-ku UGULA, 30, 144 ii 2; 30, 175c 3'

⸢Ku?-ku?-zi⸣?, 31, 418:19

Ku-ru-DINGIR(-x)?, IM 23304 rev. 6'

  [Ku?-r]u-DINGIR [s. of] SI.A-um, 32, 350:6

[Ku?-r]u-UR.SAG s. of ^{d}IM-sar, 30, 177n 1

Ku-ru-ub-Ì-la-ag šu Ì-lí-be-lí AB+ÁŠ, 30, 406 ii 5

  Ku-ru-ub-Ì-⟨la⟩-ag s. of ⸢....⸣, 30, 177h 5

Lá-[....], 31, 122 rev. i 18

Lá-a-im (gen.), 32, 345 rev. iii 12

[L]a-ʾà-ra-ab, 30, 149:2

La-bi-bu?-um, 31, 122 ii 13

La-da-k[um]?: DINGIR-ba-ni DUMU La-da-k[um? ši? M]u?-da-a?, 30, 406 rev. i 17

La-e-pum f. of Šu-ì-lí-su, 32, 346 rev. ii 6

La-gi-pum s. of Iš-má-a-ni, 30, 150:1

  [La]-gi-pum, 30, 149:1

La-mu-um: Gu-nu-núm šu La-mu-um LÚ.SIRIS, 30, 406 i 7

La-ni-m[u]?, 31, 122 rev. ii 11

Li-bur-me-šum, 30, 559c rev. 4'

[L]i?-l[i]?, 31, 122 rev. ii 5

Lu-ga-tum f. of PÙ.ŠA-^{d}EN.ZU, 30, 144 rev. ii 11

Lu-lu, 31, 134:9; 32, 527 ii 3, rev. 1

  ⸢L⸣u-lu, 32, 413 rev. 2'

Pù-ni-a šu Ša-li-ba, 30, 406 i 4

Pù-pù, 32, 347 ii 8; IM 23302:12

Pù-p[ù]?, 30, 173b ii 3

[P]ù-p[ù], 32, 359:8

⌈Pù?-pù⌉?, 30, 173a ii 6

Pù-pù AB+ÁŠ.URU^{KI}, 32, 361:4

Pù-pù SILÀ.ŠU.DU$_{8}$, 32, 358:10

Pù-pù s. of I-nin-[nu]?, 30, 177h 1

Pù-p[ù] s. of [....], 32, 345 rev. ii 11

Pù-sa-šum, IM 23302:13

Bu-BALA, 31, 143:7, 27

Pù-sar, 31, 122 rev. ii 9

PÙ.Ša-mu-sa? or PÙ.ŠA-Mu-sa?, 30, 559f 2

Pù-su-DÙG, 30, 767:3

Pù-su-su, see Pù-zu-zu

PÙ.ŠA-X, 31, 122 rev. ii 4

PÙ.ŠA-[....], 30, 767:9; 31, 122 rev. i 14

PÙ.ŠA-.[...] br. of Gu-lí-zu[m], s. of ⌈I-ku?-$^{d?}$KA⌉, 30, 144 rev. i 5

PÙ.Š[A-....], 32, 346 rev. i 1; 32, 372a 6

[PÙ]?.ŠA-[....], 30, 559d 7

PÙ.ŠA-^{d}EN.Z[U], 30, 559f 5

PÙ.ŠA-^{d}EN.ZU s. of Lu-ga-tum, 30, 144 rev. ii 10

PÙ.ŠA-Eš$_{4}$-dar, 30, 146:5

[PÙ.ŠA]?-Eš$_{4}$-dar, 31, 122 ii 23

PÙ.ŠA-Eš$_{4}$-d[ar] s. of DINGIR-a-z[u], 30, 177h 3

PÙ.ŠA-Eš$_{4}$-dar [šu? M]u?-rí-um [LÚ.MUNU$_{x}$]?.⌈G⌉Á, 30, 406 i 9

PÙ.ŠA-ḪAL, 32, 346 ii 5; 32, 413 ii 7

PÙ.ŠA-^{d}IM, 31, 133:16'; 32, 345 rev. iii 14

PÙ.ŠA-iš-su?, IM 23302:3

PÙ.ŠA-Ma-ma, 31, 143:8

[PÙ.Š]A-Ma-ma, 31, 143:10

[PÙ]?.ŠA-^{d}ME.SI, 30, 152:2

PÙ.ŠA-Mu-sa?, see Pù-Ša-mu-sa?

[PÙ.Š]A-^{d}Nisaba, 30, 152:12

[PÙ.ŠA]?-^{d}Nisaba s. of Ni-na⌈....⌉, 31, 418:28

PÙ.ŠA-^{d}Nu-ni br. of PÙ.ŠA-^{d}Za-ba_4-ba_4, s. of It-be-la-ba, 30, 144 i 9

PÙ.ŠA-⌈ru⌉-ru, 31, 122 iii 22

PÙ.ŠA-su-ni, 32, 372a 2

PÙ.ŠA-^{d}Za-ba_4-ba_4, 31, 143:9

PÙ.[ŠA]-^{d}Z[a-ba_4-ba_4], 30, 406 iii 15

PÙ.ŠA-^{d}Za-ba_4-ba_4 [DA]M.GÀR, 30, 152:19

PÙ.ŠA-^{d}Za-ba_4-ba_4 br. of PÙ.ŠA-^{d}Nu-ni, s. of It-be-la-ba, 30, 144 i 10

PÙ.ŠA-^{d}Za-ba_4-ba_4 f. of DINGIR-dan, 30, 144 i 22

Pù-zu-zu, 30, 142:5; 30, 149:4; 30, 170d 3

Pù-su-su, 32, 354:3; 32, 372a 1

Pù-zu-zu br. of? Šu-ì-lí-su, s. of? $Eš_4$-dar-BÀD-rí, 31, 121 ii 12

[Ra-b]a-tum sis. of Me-na-mu, d. of [....-š]a?, 31, 121 i 2

Ra-⌈bí⌉-DINGIR, 31, 143:25

[R]a?-ḫi-um, 31, 122 ii 22

Ra-ši-ši, 31, 122 ii 16

Rí-ig-mu-[um] f. of ^{d}IM-[....], 30, 144 rev. i 14

Rí-iṣ-DINGIR f. of SI.A-um, 32, 345 rev. iii 9
Rí-iš-tum m. of A-mur?-DÙG, 31, 121 ii 4

Sa-tu-DINGIR, 32, 346 rev. ii 2
Sa-tu-ì-lum, 30, 347b ii 3'
Sa-tu-tu PAB.PAB, 32, 350:9
Sá-ki-ki, 31, 122 iii 21
Sá-lim-[a-ḫu], 30, 142:3
  Sá-lim-a-ḫu, 30, 170b 2
  Sá-lim-a-ḫu s. of Ši-.[...], 30, 144 i 23
Sag-gul-lum, 31, 122 ii 15
Sal-ma-tum, see Mim-ma-tum
Sar-a-ti-gu-bi-si-in, 30, 170e 8
Sar-ru-ba-ni, 30, 140:17
Sar-ru-ru, 30, 144 rev. ii 1
  Sar-ru-ru: DINGIR-dan šu Ma-ga-ga ši Sar-ru-ru, 30, 406 iii 14
SI.A-um, 31, 121 rev. i 2
  [S]I.A-um, 30, 351b 3
  [SI].A-um, 31, 122 v 16
  [SI].⌈A⌉-um, 30, 170d 15
  SI.A-um s. of Rí-iṣ-DINGIR, 32, 345 rev. iii 8
  SI.A-um [f. of Ku?-r]u-DINGIR, 32, 350:6
  SI.A-⌈um⌉? f. of Zé-lí-tum, 30, 559e 2
  [SI].A-um br. of DINGIR-a-zu DUB.SAR, 30, 406 rev. ii 12
Si-du, 24, 655:3
Si-ir-ga-núm [s. of G]àr-[t]um SIPA ÁB, 30, 406 ii 16
Si-ir-ḫa-núm, 30, 140:3

Šu-ì-lí-su [SI]PA ÁB: DINGIR-su-ra-bi [šu]
Šu-ì-lí-su [SI]PA ÁB, 30, 406 rev. ii 10

Šu-ì-lí-su: DINGIR-dan ši (gen.) Šu-ì-lí-su SAG.DU$_5$ ARÁD DINGIR-ba-ni DAM.GÀR ARÁD Sar-a-ti-gu-bi-si-in (a ruler), 30, 170e 4

Šu-ì-lí-su šu LÚ.KAR, 30, 144 rev. ii 13

⌈Šu⌉-ì-lí-su šu Šu-ma-za-ba, 30, 406 ii 10

Šu-Ma-[ma], 32, 372a 5

Šu-ma-za-ba, see Su$_4$-ma-za-ba

Šu-ra?, 31, 122 rev. ii 10

Šu-^{d}Za-ba$_4$-ba$_4$ s. of Igi-sig$_7$, 30, 177g 7

Ta-ta, 32, 353:7

Tab-ba-ba: É-da-mu šu Tab-ba-ba, 30, 406 iii 4

Tab-su-ga s. of DINGIR-su-dan, 30, 144 rev. i 20

Te-mi-tum, 30, 404a 1

Te-mi-tum GEMÉ I-lul-DINGIR, ⌈s. of⌉ En-na-DINGIR, 31, 134:1

Ti-[....], 30, 144 ii 10

Ti-ga-lí, 31, 136:4'

Ti-ru-um, 30, 767:1', 1

Ti-ru-um f. of [ME]?-DINGIR, 30, 406 ii 3

Ti-⌈ti⌉?, 31, 143:20

Ti-ti f. of Zu-zu, 32, 345 rev. ii 5

U-ba-ru-um, 30, 144 rev. i 17

[U]-ba-ru-um, 31, 122 iii 19

U-[b]ar-ru-u[m], 30, 144 ii 23

U-ba-ru-um s. of [A]-ḫu-mu-bí, 30, 559d 5

U-ba-ru-um s. of A-mur-^{d}UTU, 30, 144 ii 14

U-da, 32, 347 i 7

[U]-za-si-⌈na-at⌉, 31, 122 ii 7

Ú-da-ad-ba-lí-il, 32, 347 ii 3

Ú-gul-la-ni-su LÚ.U_x(GIŠGAL), 30, 170c 10

Ú-KA-li, 32, 358:4

Ú-lu-[....], 32, 372d 6'

Ù-ì-lí, 30, 150:5, 6; 32, 348 i 4', 11'; 32, 527 ii 6, 15

Ù-ù, 32, 413 ii 5

Ub-da f. of Ì-la-ag-nu-id, 30, 177n 6

[Um]-mi-$Eš_4$-dar ⌈s. of⌉ DINGIR-ga-lí, 30, 144 i 6

UN.Í[L], 31, 122 iv 20

Ur-[....], 30, 767:8; 31, 122 iii 8

Ur-.[...], 31, 122 iii 9

Ur?-[....], 31, 122 iii 17

Ur-barag, 24, 661:2

Ur-^{d}En-ki, 24, 655:6

⌈U⌉r-^{d}I[M]?, 31, 122 rev. i 12

Ur-^{d}KA.DI, 24, 689:3

[Ur]-^{d}KA.DI, 31, 133:14'

Ur-⌈Keš⌉?^{KI}, 31, 122 ii 12

Ur-kisal, 32, 357:2

Ur-maḫ?, 32, 347 i 2

Ur-pisan NU.SAR, 24, 661:9, 14

Ur-s[ag-x], 31, 122 iii 16

Ur-si-gar, 31, 121 rev. i 4

Ur-$ša_6$, 24, 680:11

Ur-$ša_6$ ⌈LÚ⌉?.GIŠ.NI, 24, 663:8

[....]-ad, 31, 122 i 22

.[...]-al-[su]?, 31, 418:23

[....]-ba [f. of? ...].-su, 30, 406:16

[...].-da?-ad?, 32, 347 i 6

[....]-dan?, 30, 406 rev. iii 3

[....-D]I.TAR [UGULA], 30, 406 rev. iii 5

[....]-DINGIR, 31, 122 i 23

[...].-DINGIR ŠU.ḪA, 30, 144 rev. ii 5

[....]-DINGIR šu Im_x(DU)-da-lik DUMU ši A-tu-tu, 30, 406 rev. ii 2

X-é-ni-šè, 31, 122 rev. i 8

[....]-GAL?, 31, 122 i 5

[....]-⌈d⌉KA, 31, 122 i 4

[....-K]A?, 31, 122 i 24

⌈....⌉-ki-ág?, 31, 122 ii 10

[....]-la, 31, 133:15'

[....-LU]GAL?, 30, 559c rev. 1'

[....LU]GAL? ⌈f. of⌉ DINGIR-ra-bí, gf. of ⌈ì⌉-lí-a-bí, 30, 559e 5

[....-L]UM, 31, 122 iii 18

[...].-mu-bí, 32, 413 ii 3

[....]-NI [s. of? B]u?-du_8-um, 30, 151:1

[....]-rí-DINGIR, 31, 418:18

[...].-sa?-ma-[x]?, 31, 143:16

[....]-⌈SIPA-ì⌉ (f.n.), 31, 121 ii 8

[...].-su [s. of? ....]-ba, 30, 406 i 15

⌈....⌉-su-rí-ik, 31, 122 rev. ii 6

[....-š]a? (f.n.) m. of [Ra-b]a-tum and Me-na-mu, 31, 121 i 1

[....]-tim?, 31, 122 i 3

[....-u]m s. of? [It-be]?-la-ba [ši? Ì-l]í?-a-ḫi, 30, 406 i 12

[....]-UŠ [SABR]A.É, 31, 130 ii 4'

2. Divine Names

A-mur-ru, see PN A-mur-ru-⸢ki?-m]a?-DINGIR

Ba-lí-il, see possibly PN Ú-da-ad-ba-lí-il

Bu, see ^{d}KA

É-a, see PNs ARÁD-É-a, BALA-É-a, É-a-dan, É-a-DÙG, É-a-ì-lí, ⸢É⸣-a-ni-⸢sá⸣, ⸢É-a⸣-ra-bí, É-a-rí-zi, É-a-sar, É-a-UR.SAG, Ga-la-ab-É-a, I-mi-É-a, I-šim-É-a, I-ti-É-a

^{d}En-ki, 30, 143:1; 31, 121 rev. i 11; see also PN Ur-^{d}En-ki

^{d}En-líl, 24, 661:6; see also PN Šu-^{d}En-líl

^{d}EN.ZU, 30, 143:18; see also PNs Be-lí-^{d}EN.ZU, È-mi-^{d}EN.ZU, I-mi-^{d}EN.ZU, ^{d}EN.ZU-al-su, ^{d}EN.ZU-iš-da-<gal>, ^{d}EN.ZU-ni-⸢sá⸣, I-da-^{d}EN.ZU, Im-gu[r-^{d}]EN.ZU, Iš-má-^{d}EN.ZU, Ki-bí-^{d}EN.ZU, Na-bí-^{d}EN.ZU, PÙ.ŠA-^{d}EN.ZU

Eš$_4$-dar, see PNs Eš$_4$-[da]r-ba-luḫ, Eš$_4$-dar-BÀD-rí, Eš$_4$-dar-dan, Eš$_4$-dar-É, Eš$_4$-dar-ni-sa, Eš$_4$-dar-nu-id, Iš-má-Eš$_4$-dar, PÙ.ŠA-Eš$_4$-dar, [Um]-mi-Eš$_4$-dar

^{d}Ḫa-ri-im, see PN ^{d}⸢Ḫa?-rí⸣-im-be-lí

Ì-la-ag, see PNs Ì-la-ag-nu-id etc., Ku-ru-ub-Ì-la-ag

^{d}IM, see PNs ^{d}IM-[....], ^{d}IM-sar, Me-iḫ-r[í-^{d}]IM,

PÙ.ŠA-^{d}IM, ⌈U⌉r-^{d}I[M]?

^{d}Innin, 30, 143:3, 33; see also PNs I-nin-DINGIR, I-nin-la-ba

^{d}Ìr-ra, see PN I-ku-^{d}Ìr-ra

^{d}Iš-ḫa-ra, 30, 143:33

^{d}KA, see PN ⌈I-ku?-$^{d?}$KA⌉, ^{d}K[A-....], ^{d}KA-Me-ir, [....]-$^{⌈d⌉}$KA

Bu, see PN Bu-bala

Pù, see PN Pù-sar

^{d}KA.DI, see PN Ur-^{d}KA.DI

Ma-ma, see PNs PÙ.ŠA-Ma-ma, Šu-Ma-[ma]

^{d}ME.SI, see PN [PÙ]?.ŠA-^{d}ME.SI

^{d}Nanše, see PN I-bí-^{d}Nanše

^{d}Nin-SAR, see PN ME-^{d}Nin-SAR

^{d}Nin-su-AN, see PN ME-^{d}Nin-su-AN

^{d}Nisaba, see PN [PÙ.Š]A-^{d}Nisaba

^{d}Nu-ni, see PN PÙ.ŠA-^{d}Nu-ni

Pù, see ^{d}KA

^{d}ŠEŠ.KI, see PN ^{d}ŠE[Š.KI-....]

Ú, see PN Ú-ì-lí

Ú-gul-la, see PN Ú-gul-la-ni-su

^{d}UTU, see PNs A-mur-^{d}UTU, ⌈Ur⌉-^{d}⌈Utu⌉, $^{⌈d⌉}$Utu-ki-ág, ^{d}UTU-li-din

^{d}Za-ba$_4$-ba$_4$, see PNs I-bí-^{d}Za-ba$_4$-ba$_4$, PÙ.ŠA-^{d}Za-ba$_4$-ba$_4$, Šu-^{d}Za-ba$_4$-ba$_4$

3. Geographic Names

A-ga-dè^{KI}, 31, 418:13, 34

CATALOGUE OF TABLETS

Tablet from Kish 1927 (No. 1)

1. Kish 1927, 1 — Data about color, size, and present location of the tablet unknown. Text published previously by Langdon, RA XXIV (1927), pp. 90f. and 96. Letter of Qibî-Sin to Ilis̆-takal.

Tablet from Kish 1929, in the Ashmolean Museum (No. 2)

2. Kish 1929, 160 — Light brown. 73 × 50 × 22 mm. Locus: Mound Z. Text published previously by Langdon, EK III Pl. XI. The first signs in lines 11-13, copied by Langdon, are now effaced on the tablet. Letter of Abbaja to Dudua. Plate I.

Tablets from Kish 1930, in the Ashmolean Museum (Nos. 3-54)

3. Kish 1930, 138 — Light brown. 56 × 42 × 18 mm. Locus: Y? Payment of one hundred and fifty gur of barley. Plate II.

4. Kish 1930, 139 Light brown. 57 × 43 × 14 mm. Locus: Y? Assignment of four individuals to two places. Plate II.

5. Kish 1930, 140 Light brown. 71 × 47 × 16 mm. Locus: Y? List of eleven individuals said to be *al* "upon" eleven other individuals. Plate I.

6. Kish 1930, 141 Light brown. 32 × 28 × 9 mm. Locus: YW? Receipt of barley. Plate II.

7. Kish 1930, 142 Light brown. 50 × 41 × 18 mm. Locus: Y? Lower part of the tablet destroyed. Assignment of nine workers to one place. Plate II.

8. Kish 1930, 143+175h Light brown. 87 × 46 × 11 mm. Locus: Y? Incantation invoking *irʾemum* "love-magic." Plates III and IV, enlarged.

9. Kish 1930, 144a+b+c Light brown. 118 × 80 × 15 mm. Locus: Y? Two-column tablet reconstructed from three frag-

ments. Rations of barley and distribution of silver to about forty-five individuals, of whom apparently only thirty-eight are included in the totals. Plate V.

10.	Kish 1930, 145	Light brown. 58 × 43 × 10 mm. Locus: Y? Disposition of animals, barley, salt, objects, and a slave-girl in three places. Plate VI.
11.	Kish 1930, 146	Light brown. 45 × 40 × 17 mm. Locus: Y? Assignment of thirty-two workers to four foremen. Plate VI.
12.	Kish 1930, 147+ 175f +175g	Light brown. 94 × 53 × 20 mm. Locus: Y? Location of ten very large fields in ten places. The total amounts to 3,132 IKU. Plate VII.
13.	Kish 1930, 148	Light brown. 58 × 42 × 18 mm. Locus: Y? Assignment of six workers to four foremen. Plate VII.

14.	Kish 1930, 149	Light brown. 51 × 40 × 13 mm. Locus: Y? List of five messengers under one foreman. Plate VI.
15.	Kish 1930, 150	Light brown. 52 × 43 × 11 mm. Locus: Y? Bottom of tablet destroyed. List of fifteen workers called <u>wa-si-bu</u> "squatters" under one foreman. Cf. Kish 1930, 177n. Plate IX.
16.	Kish 1930, 151	Light brown. 40 × 37 × 13 mm. Locus: YWN. Assignment of two (or four?) workers to A.ḪA^{KI}. Plate VIII.
17.	Kish 1930, 152	Light brown. 87 × 47 × 17 mm. Locus: Y? Receipt of barley (instead of silver) by nine <u>bêlū</u> "lords." Cf. also Kish IM 23302 end. Plate VIII.
18.	Kish 1930, 170a	Light brown. 70 × 48 × 18 mm. Assignment of two hundred and seventeen workers to thirteen foremen. Plate IX.
19.	Kish 1930, 170b	Light brown. 61 × 43 × 16 mm.

List of six fugitive workers. Plate VII.

20. Kish 1930, 170c Light brown. 51 × 48 × 14 mm. Letter of Eštar-paluḫ to one or two individuals. Plate X.

21. Kish 1930, 170d Light brown. 41 × 32 × 12 mm. Witnessed loan of barley by Adad-šar from Puzuzu. Plate X.

22. Kish 1930, 170e Light brown. 38 × 29 × 11 mm. Order to return a man dwelling with Ilum-dan. Plate X.

23. Kish 1930, 170f Light brown. 37 × 30 × 15 mm. Bottom of tablet destroyed, but perhaps no more than one line missing. Disposition of silver, gold, garments, bronze vessels, etc. Plate XI.

24. Kish 1930, 170g Light brown. 30 × 27 × 13 mm. Receipt of barley by Naḫšum-palaʾ from Iliš-takal. Plate XI.

25. Kish 1930, 173a Light brown. 37 × 38 × 20 mm. Locus: Y Red Stratum. Thick, roundish tablet. Distribution

of sheep. Text similar to Kish 1930, 173a. Plate XII.

27. Kish 1930, 173c Light brown. 57 × 32 × 19 mm. Locus: Y 2 m. Red Stratum. Fragment of a thick, roundish tablet. Destroyed but for one sign É. Plate XII.

28. Kish 1930, 175b Light brown. 34 × 38 × 16 mm. Bottom of tablet destroyed. List of four messengers under four foremen. Text similar to Kish 1930, 175c. Plate XII.

29. Kish 1930, 175c Light brown. 35 × 46 × 18 mm. Top of tablet destroyed. List of messengers? under foremen. Text similar to Kish 1930, 175b. Plate XII.

30. Kish 1930, 175e Light brown. 25 × 37 × 13 mm. Top of tablet destroyed. Several loans of silver. Plate XIII.

31. Kish 1930, 175i Light brown. 37 × 42 × 6 mm. Top of tablet destroyed, reverse of tablet flaked off.

Account of barley. Plate XIII.

32. Kish 1930, 175j Light brown. 50 × 32 × 8 mm. Left and right sides of tablet destroyed. Reverse of tablet flaked off. Contents undefinable. Plate XIII.

33. Kish 1930, 177g Light brown. 73 × 33 × 25 mm. Left and bottom of tablet destroyed. To judge from the greater thickness of the tablet on the left side, in comparison with the lesser thickness on the right side, the preserved part constitutes column ii of the tablet. List of messengers? under foremen. Cf. the similar text Kish 1930, 175b. Plate XIII.

34. Kish 1930, 177h Light brown. 34 × 44 × 20 mm. Bottom of tablet destroyed. List of fourteen workers under one foreman. Plate XIV.

35. Kish 1930, 177k Light brown. 45 × 45 × 13 mm. Fragment of a two-column tablet. Reverse flaked off. Contents undefinable. Plate XIII.

36. Kish 1930, 177n Light brown. 81 × 40 × 21 mm. Right side of tablet destroyed. List of workers called wa-si-bu "squatters." Cf. Kish 1930, 150. Plate XIV.

37. Kish 1930, 345d Reddish-brown. 33 × 33 × 10 mm. Locus: C 6, 2 m. Reverse uninscribed. Unreadable signs. School text. Plate XIV.

38. Kish 1930, 347b Light brown. 32 × 45 × 11 mm. Locus: C 6, 4 m. Round tablet. Top of tablet destroyed. Contents undefinable. Plate XV.

39. Kish 1930, 348b Reddish-brown. 85 × 40 × 23 mm. Locus: C 6, 7 m. Only left side of tablet preserved. Contents undefinable. Plate XV.

40. Kish 1930, 349b Reddish-brown. 40 × 42 × 13 mm. Locus: C 6, PL. Bottom of tablet destroyed. Text deals with a field. Plate XV.

41. Kish 1930, 351b Light brown. 21 × 24 × 11 mm. Locus: C 5, 3 m. Bottom of tablet destroyed. Account of

		sheep and goats. Plate XV.
42.	Kish 1930, 399a	Light brown. 26 × 22 × 11 mm. Locus: C 7, 4 m. Writing badly worn. Account of goats. Plate XVI.
43.	Kish 1930, 403	Light brown. 37 × 40 × 18 mm. Locus: C 7, PL. Roundish tablet. Beginning of a two-column uncompleted tablet. Account of flour. Plate XV.
44.	Kish 1930, 404a	Light brown. 32 × 28 × 7 mm. Locus: YWN. Distribution of barley for one individual and one pig. Plate XVI.
45.	Kish 1930, 406	Light to reddish-brown. 91 × 81 × 20 mm. Locus: YWN, 0.50 m. Three-column tablet. Account of workers, dead and fugitive, in one year in a place called Šitul-nišē. Plate XVII.
46.	Kish 1930, 559a	Reddish-brown. 39 × 32 × 12 mm. List of workers called _za-bi-ù gi-nu-tum_. Plate XVI.

47. Kish 1930, 559b Light brown. 37 × 31 × 12 mm. Locus: YWN. Roundish in appearance. Contents undefinable. Distribution of one item each to three individuals. Plate XVIII.

48. Kish 1930, 559c Dark gray. 42 × 45 × 22 mm. Top and bottom destroyed. Witnessed contract concerning the purchase of a field. Plate XVIII.

49. Kish 1930, 559d Light brown. 59 × 33 × 12 mm. Top of reverse destroyed. Contents undefinable. List of men. Plate XVIII.

50. Kish 1930, 559e Brown-gray. 35 × 35 × 12 mm. Bottom of tablet destroyed. Contents undefinable. List of women. Plate XVIII.

51. Kish 1930, 559f Brown-gray. 55 × 49 × 22 mm. Bottom of tablet destroyed. Contents undefinable. List of men. Plate XIX.

52. Kish 1930, 766 Light brown. 57 × 42 × 21 mm.

		Only upper right part of tablet preserved. Account of barley. Plate XIX.
53.	Kish 1930, 767	Light brown. 63 × 39 × 13 mm. Obverse (flat) flaked off. Contents undefinable. List of men. Plate XIX.
54.	Kish 1930, 768	Very light to light brown. 48 × 35 × 14 mm. Letter of Warassuni to Tašmaᶜtum concerning two fugitives. Plate XIX.

Tablets from Kish 1931, in the Ashmolean Museum (Nos. 55-65)

55.	Kish 1931, 86	Light brown. 32 × 42 × 22 mm. Top of obverse destroyed. Account of sheep and goats. Plate XXVI.
56.	Kish 1931, 121	Light brown. 95 × 100 × 23 mm. Three-column tablet. List of thirty-seven GURUŠ and GEMÉ in the household of ^{d}En-ki. Plate XX.
57.	Kish 1931, 122	Light brown. 141 × 143 × 25 mm.

		Locus: C 10 (5). Five-column tablet. Text difficult to read. List of one hundred and thirty-eight male individuals. Plates XXI and XXII.
58.	Kish 1931, 130	Light brown. 117 × 73 × 27 mm. Large fragment of a two (or more) column tablet. To judge from the context, probably the reverse of the tablet. Obverse almost completely flaked off. List of GURUŠ under foremen. Plate XXIII.
59.	Kish 1931, 133	Reddish-brown. 54 × 50 × 20 mm. Only right side of tablet preserved. The attempted reconstruction of the beginnings of the lines is based on the thickness of the tablet. Account of barley. Plate XXIV.
60.	Kish 1931, 134	Reddish-brown. 33 × 30 × 8 mm. Memorandum about a slave-girl and two or three persons. Plate XXIV.
61.	Kish 1931, 136	Reddish-brown. 58 × 40 × 25 mm.

Fragment. All edges destroyed. Distribution of fish, flour, etc. Plate XXV.

62. Kish 1931, 143 Light and reddish-brown. 72 × 47 × 16 mm. Left edge is broken away so that it is impossible to see clearly how much is missing in front of the preserved portions of the lines. List of personal names. Plate XXV.

63. Kish 1931, 144a Light gray. 33 × 30 × 11 mm. Locus: YWN .01 m. Account of wool and lambs. Plate XXVI.

64. Kish 1931, 144c Light brown. 30 × 48 × 12 mm. Locus: C 7 or YWN .01 m. Fragment of an at least three-column tablet. Reverse flaked off. Epigraphically, the text appears to be older than others in this collection. Writing GUR ŠE GÁL SAG, for the standard Sargonic ŠE GUR.SAG.GÁL, is unique. Account of barley. Plate XXIV.

65. Kish 1931, 418 Dark brown. 85 × 42 × 22 mm. Witnessed contract concerning the purchase of a field. Plate XXVI.

Tablets from Umm-el-Jīr 1932, in the Ashmolean Museum (Nos. 66-101)

66. Umm-el-Jīr 1932, 345 Reddish-brown. 97 × 106 × 24 mm. Three-column tablet. Memo concerning the witnessed receipt of barley (silver and other commodities) for thirteen fields, two loans, and three houses by twenty individuals; apparently a composite memo concerning different transactions of one unnamed individual or household. Plates XXVII and XXVIII.

67. Umm-el-Jīr 1932, 346 Light reddish-brown. 103 × 78 × 17 mm. Two-column tablet. List of fourteen very large fields in fourteen locations with the names of their owners.

The fields total 1,830 IKU. Plate XXIX.

68.	Umm-el-Jīr 1932, 347	Light reddish-brown. 85 × 85 × 20 mm. Three-column tablet. Reverse uninscribed. Memo about small amounts of barley for the feeding of the household. Plate XXX.
69.	Umm-el-Jīr 1932, 348	Light reddish-brown. 87 × 65 × 20 mm. Left side of an at least three-column tablet. Obverse flat, reverse flaked off. Account of different commodities. Cf. note on the parallel text Umm-el-Jīr 1932, 527. Plate XXXI.
70.	Umm-el-Jīr 1932, 349	Light reddish-brown. 48 × 32 × 15 mm. Receipt of small amounts of barley by four persons from two persons. Plate XXVII.
71.	Umm-el-Jīr 1932, 350	Light brown. 43 × 29 × 12 mm. Delivery of large

		amounts of barley by two persons. Plate XXVIII.
72.	Umm-el-Jīr 1932, 351	Reddish-brown. 48 × 32 × 14 mm. Receipt of barley by one man as price of his son, and receipt of barley by one woman as price of a field. Plate XXX.
73.	Umm-el-Jīr 1932, 352	Reddish-brown. 55 × 38 × 16 mm. Account of different commodities and implements. Plate XXXI.
74.	Umm-el-Jīr 1932, 353	Light brown. 60 × 43 × 17 mm. Issue on loan of small amounts of barley by seven persons. Text similar to Umm-el-Jīr 1932, 356. Plate XXXI.
75.	Umm-el-Jīr 1932, 354	Very light brown. 50 × 35 × 15 mm. Obverse flat, covered by a seal impression showing a lion fighting a goat; revers (with inscription) round. Letter of Zuzu to Puzuzu

		concerning bronze. Cf. Umm-el-Jīr 1932, 360. Plate XXXII.
76.	Umm-el-Jīr 1932, 355	Reddish-brown. 47 × 35 × 18 mm. Issue of sixty-one goats. Plate XXXII.
77.	Umm-el-Jīr 1932, 356	Reddish-brown. 41 × 30 × 18 mm. Issue on loan of small amounts of barley by two persons. Text similar to Umm-el-Jīr 1932, 353. Plate XXXII.
78.	Umm-el-Jīr 1932, 357	Light brown. 40 × 34 × 13 mm. Receipt on loan of large amount of barley by one person. Plate XXXIII.
79.	Umm-el-Jīr 1932, 358	Reddish-brown. 42 × 28 × 16 mm. Account of barley. Plate XXXIII.
80.	Umm-el-Jīr 1932, 359	Reddish-brown. 52 × 35 × 13 mm. Delivery of barley by four persons. Plate XXXIII.
81.	Umm-el-Jīr 1932, 360	Reddish-brown. 35 × 30 × 13

mm. Letter of Zuzu to Šaṭpum concerning barley. Cf. Umm-el-Jīr 1932, 354. Plate XXXIII.

82.	Umm-el-Jīr 1932, 361	Reddish-brown. 33 × 27 × 12 mm. Receipt of barley as price of a house. Plate XXXIV.
83.	Umm-el-Jīr 1932, 362	Reddish-brown. 28 × 25 × 10 mm. Since, exceptionally, both sides are round, there is no way to distinguish the obverse from the reverse. Letter from Šūma-ṣabaʾ to Šuliʾum concerning the watering of a field. Plate XXXIV.
84.	Umm-el-Jīr 1932, 363	Reddish-brown. 35 × 25 × 12 mm. Receipt of silver, sheep, and barley by one man and his mother. Plate XXXIV.
85.	Umm-el-Jīr 1932, 364	Reddish-brown. 42 × 33 × 15 mm. Issue of a very large amount of barley to be used for bread of the household. Text unfinished. Plate XXXV.

86.	Umm-el-Jīr 1932, 365	Reddish-brown. 33 × 31 × 10 mm. Both sides roundish. Memo concerning large amount of silver borrowed by one person. Cf. Umm-el-Jīr 1932, 367. Plate XXXV.
87.	Umm-el-Jīr 1932, 366	Reddish-brown. 40 × 30 × 16 mm. Account of barley. Plate XXXV.
88.	Umm-el-Jīr 1932, 367	Reddish-brown. 40 × 38 × 13 mm. Receipt of silver, and issue of barley. Cf. Umm-el-Jīr 1932, 365. Plate XXXVI.
89.	Umm-el-Jīr 1932, 368	Light brown. 48 × 50 × 18 mm. Bulky form. Possibly a school exercise. Plate XXXVI.
90.	Umm-el-Jīr 1932, 369	Light brown. 37 × 35 × 16 mm. Roundish tablet. Probably a school exercise. Signs crossed out. Plate XXXVI.

91.	Umm-el-Jīr 1932, 370	Light reddish-brown. 67 × 65 × 17 mm. Circular (not four-sided) tablet. Obverse flat, reverse rounded. Writing on the reverse is oriented sideways in relation to the obverse. School exercise. Plate XXXVII.
92.	Umm-el-Jīr 1932, 372a	Five fragments, all Sargonic, not related. Largest fragment: Light brown. 40 × 40 × 11 mm. Obverse flat, reverse flaked off. Account of rations? of barley? Plate XXXVI.
93.	Umm-el-Jīr 1932, 372b	Light brown. 23 × 31 × 5 mm. A very small fragment. Reverse flaked off. Account of barley. Plate XXXVII.
94.	Umm-el-Jīr 1932, 372c	Light reddish-brown. 18 × 14 × 3 mm. A very small fragment. Reverse flaked off. Contents undefinable. Plate XXXVII.

95. Umm-el-Jīr 1932, 372d — Light brown. 28 × 20 × 18 mm. A small fragment. Account of barley? Plate XXXVIII.

96. Umm-el-Jīr 1932, 372e — Light brown. Reverse flaked off. Worthless fragment. Only BÍ visible. Plate XXXVII.

97. Umm-el-Jīr? 1932, 402 — Reddish-brown. 67 × 40 × 16 mm. Reverse flaked off. Distribution of barley for various purposes. Plate XXXVII.

98. Umm-el-Jīr 1932, 413 — Light brown. 58 × 47 × 26 mm. Left and bottom sides destroyed. At least two columns. Account of barley. Plate XXXVIII.

99. Umm-el-Jīr? 1932, 416 — Reddish-brown. 45 × 43 × 18 mm. Lower part of tablet destroyed. Account of fields with their measurements. Plate XXXVIII.

100.	Umm-el-Jīr 1932, 420	Light reddish-brown. 43 × 37 × 14 mm. Account of wooden objects and sheep. Plate XXXIX.
101.	Umm-el-Jīr 1932, 527	Light reddish-brown. 96 × 61 × 17 mm. At least two columns. Left side destroyed. Account of different commodities. Same color, same size of signs, and same contents as Umm-el-Jīr 1932, 348, but the two large fragments cannot be joined and must represent two different tablets. Plate XXXIX.

Tablets from Kish 1935?, in the Iraq Museum (Nos. 102-104)

102.	Kish IM 23302	Brown. 63 × 41 × 18 mm. Receipt of silver by several *bêlū* "lords." Cf. also Kish 1930, 152 end.
103.	Kish IM 23304	Gray-brown. 63 × 40 × 18 mm. Bottom and right

		edge of obverse destroyed. Distribution of barley to women.
104.	Kish IM 23305	Light brown. 42 × 32 × 17 mm. Issue of barley for various purposes.

Tablets of Unknown Origin, in the Ashmolean Museum (Nos. 105-113)

105.	Ashmolean 1924, 655	Reddish-brown. 65 × 48 × 17 mm. Memo about the exchange of four fields owned by four individuals for oxen. Plate XL.
106.	Ashmolean 1924, 661	Light brown. 92 × 48 × 16 mm. Record of fourteen orchards, with their date-palms, owners, and/or gardeners. Plate XLI.
107.	Ashmolean 1924, 662	Light brown. 74 × 40 × 13 mm. Record of different kinds of flour assigned to five persons. Plate XL.
108.	Ashmolean 1924, 663	Light brown. 66 × 43 × 13 mm. Distribution of

		barley, silver, and sheep to five persons. Plate XLII.
109.	Ashmolean 1924, 664	Light brown. 38 × 34 × 13 mm. Delivery of BAPPIR to the É.ÙR. Plate XLI.
110.	Ashmolean 1924, 680	Reddish-brown. 62 × 46 × 17 mm. Inventory of an individual. Plate XLII.
111.	Ashmolean 1924, 684	Reddish-brown. 55 × 43 × 17 mm. Account of barley of two persons in Giršu. Plate XLIII.
112.	Ashmolean 1924, 689	Reddish-brown. 48 × 45 × 13 mm. Description of an area of 500,000 IKU = about 200,000 hectars = 2,000 square kilometers. The text yields immense areas and is ununderstandable to me. Plate XLIII.
113.	Ashmolean 1924, 692	Reddish-brown. 54 × 42 × 13 mm. Receipt of different kinds of flour by two persons. Plate XLIII.

PLATES

2. (Kish 1929, 160)

5. (Kish 1930, 140)

PLATE II

3. (Kish 1930, 138)

6. (Kish 1930, 141)

4. (Kish 1930, 139)

7. (Kish 1930, 142)

8. (Kish 1930, 143+175h) obv.

PLATE IV

8. (Kish 1930, 143+175h) rev.

9. (Kish 1930, 144a+b+c)

PLATE VI

10. (Kish 1930, 145)

11. (Kish 1930, 146)

14. (Kish 1930, 149)

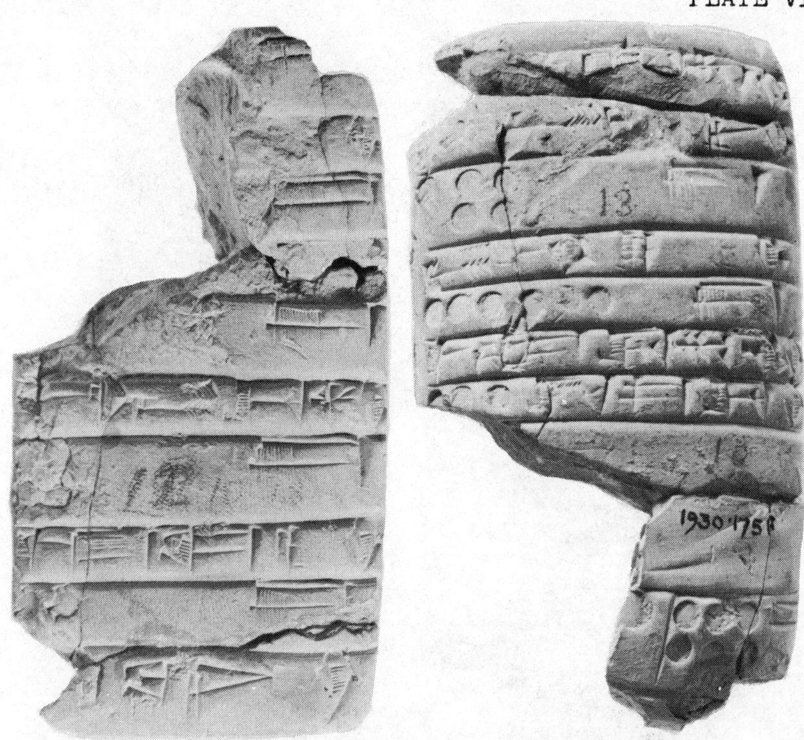

12. (Kish 1930, 147+175f+175g)

13. (Kish 1930, 148)

19. (Kish 1930, 170b)

PLATE VIII

16. (Kish 1930, 151)

17. (Kish 1930, 152)

15. (Kish 1930, 150)

18. (Kish 1930, 170a)

PLATE X

20. (Kish 1930, 170c)

21. (Kish 1930, 170d)

22. (Kish 1930, 170e)

PLATE XI

23. (Kish 1930, 170f)

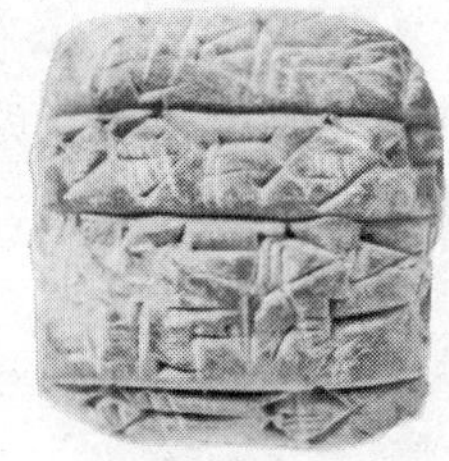

24. (Kish 1930, 170g)

25. (Kish 1930, 173a)

PLATE XII

26. (Kish 1930, 173b)

27. (Kish 1930, 173c)

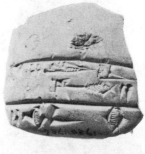

28. (Kish 1930, 175b)

29. (Kish 1930, 175c)

30. (Kish 1930, 175e)

31. (Kish 1930, 175i)

32. (Kish 1930, 175j)

35. (Kish 1930, 177k)

33. (Kish 1930, 177g)

PLATE XIV

34. (Kish 1930, 177h)

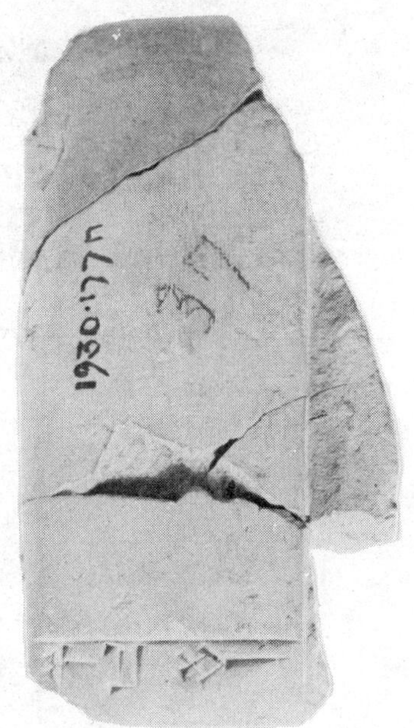

36. (Kish 1930, 177n)

37. (Kish 1930, 345d)

PLATE XV

38. (Kish 1930, 347b)

40. (Kish 1930, 349b)

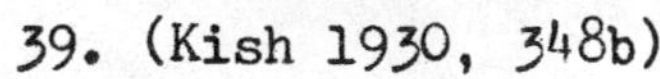

39. (Kish 1930, 348b)

41. (Kish 1930, 351b)

43. (Kish 1930, 403)

PLATE XVI

42. (Kish 1930, 399a)

44. (Kish 1930, 404a)

46. (Kish 1930, 559a)

45. (Kish 1930, 406)

PLATE XVIII

47. (Kish 1930, 559b)

48. (Kish 1930, 559c)

49. (Kish 1930, 559d)   50. (Kish 1930, 559e)

PLATE XIX

51. (Kish 1930, 559f)

52. (Kish 1930, 766)

53. (Kish 1930, 767)

54. (Kish 1930, 768)

PLATE XX

56. (Kish 1931, 121)

57. (Kish 1931, 122) obv. [reduced]

PLATE XXII

57. (Kish 1931, 122) rev. [reduced]

PLATE XXIII

58. (Kish 1931, 130)

PLATE XXIV

55. (Kish 1931, 86)

64. (Kish 1931, 144c)

59. (Kish 1931, 133)

60. (Kish 1931, 134)

PLATE XXV

61. (Kish 1931, 136)

62. (Kish 1931, 143)

63. (Kish 1931, 144a)

65. (Kish 1931, 418)

66. (Umm-el-Jīr 1932, 345) obv.

70. (Umm-el-Jīr 1932, 349)

66. (Umm-el-Jīr 1932, 345) rev.

71. (Umm-el-Jīr 1932, 350)

67. (Umm-el-Jīr 1932, 346)

68. (Umm-el-Jīr 1932, 347)

72. (Umm-el-Jīr 1932, 351)

73. (Umm-el-Jīr 1932, 352)

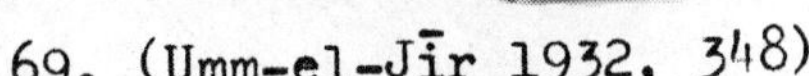

69. (Umm-el-Jīr 1932, 348)

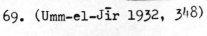

74. (Umm-el-Jīr 1932, 353)

PLATE XXXII

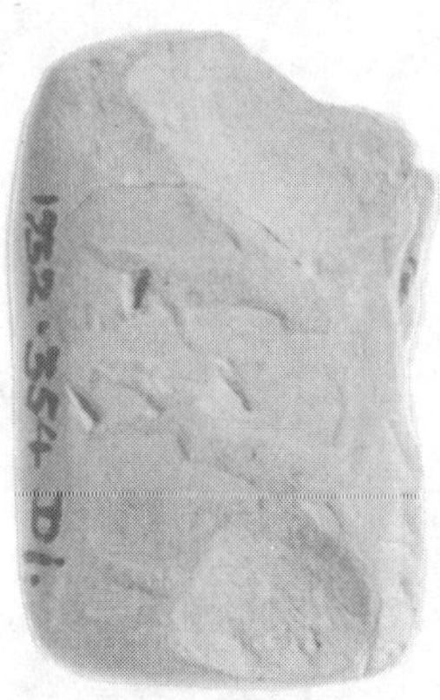

75. (Umm-el-Jīr 1932, 354)

76. (Umm-el-Jīr 1932, 355)

77. (Umm-el-Jīr 1932, 356)

PLATE XXXIII

78. (Umm-el-Jīr 1932, 357)

81. (Umm-el-Jīr 1932, 360)

79. (Umm-el-Jīr 1932, 358)

80. (Umm-el-Jīr 1932, 359)

PLATE XXXIV

82. (Umm-el-Jīr 1932, 361)

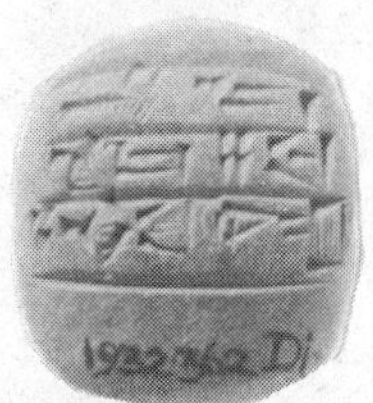

83. (Umm-el-Jīr 1932, 362)

84. (Umm-el-Jīr 1932, 363)

85. (Umm-el-Jīr 1932, 364)

86. (Umm-el-Jīr 1932, 365)

87. (Umm-el-Jīr 1932, 366)

PLATE XXXVI

88. (Umm-el-Jīr 1932, 367)

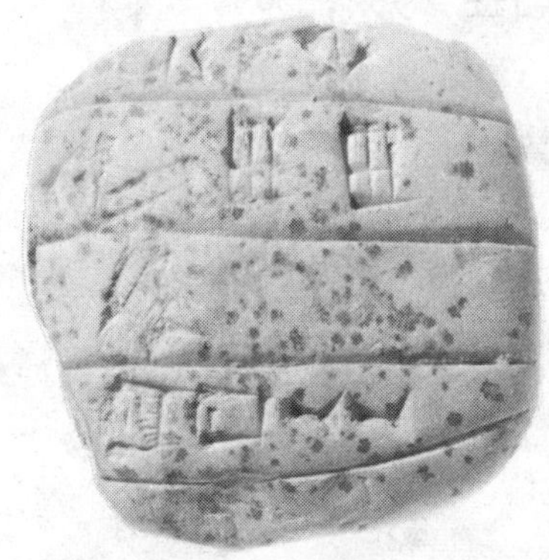

92. (Umm-el-Jīr 1932, 372a)

89. (Umm-el-Jīr 1932, 368)

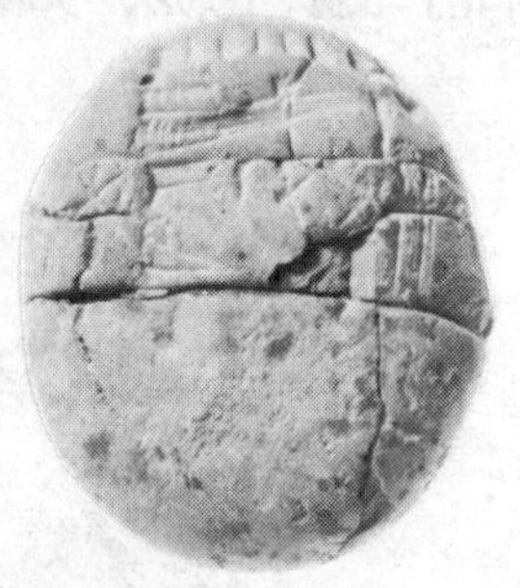

90. (Umm-el-Jīr 1932, 369)

91. (Umm-el-Jīr 1932, 370)

93. (Umm-el-Jīr 1932, 372b)

94. (Umm-el-Jīr 1932, 372c)

96. (Umm-el-Jīr 1932, 372e)

97. (Umm-el-Jīr 1932, 402)

PLATE XXXVIII

95. (Umm-el-Jīr 1932, 372d)

98. (Umm-el-Jīr 1932, 413)

99. (Umm-el-Jīr 1932, 416)

100. (Umm-el-Jīr 1932, 420)

101. (Umm-el-Jīr 1932, 527)

105. (Ashm. 1924, 655)

107. (Ashm. 1924, 662)

PLATE XLI

106. (Ashm. 1924, 661)

109. (Ashm. 1924, 664)

PLATE XLII

108. (Ashm. 1924, 663)

110. (Ashm. 1924, 680)

111. (Ashm. 1924, 684)

112. (Ashm. 1924, 689)

113. (Ashm. 1924, 692)

PLATE XLIV

2. (Kish 1929, 160) obv.

60. (Kish 1931, 134) rev.

39. (Kish 1930, 348b) obv.

65. (Kish 1931, 418) obv.

47. (Kish 1930, 559b) obv.

PLATE XLV

45. (Kish 1930, 406)

PLATE XLVI

114. (Ashm. 1969, 562)

115. (Ashm. 1969, 563)

116. (Ashm. 1969, 564)